The Sea Hawk

Wisconsin/Warner Bros. Screenplay Series

The Sea Hawk

Edited with an introduction by

Rudy Behlmer

Published for the Wisconsin Center for Film and Theater Research by
The University of Wisconsin Press

Published 1982

The University of Wisconsin Press
114 North Murray Street
Madison, Wisconsin 53715

The University of Wisconsin Press, Ltd.
1 Gower Street
London WC1E 6HA, England

First printing

Printed in the United States of America

For LC CIP information see the colophon

ISBN 0-299-09010-8 cloth; 0-299-09014-0 paper

Publication of this volume has been assisted by a grant from
The Brittingham Fund, Inc.

Contents

Foreword

In donating the Warner Film Library to the Wisconsin Center for Film and Theater Research in 1969, along with the RKO and Monogram film libraries and UA corporate records, United Artists created a truly great resource for the study of American film. Acquired by United Artists in 1957, during a period when the major studios sold off their films for use on television, the Warner library is by far the richest portion of the gift, containing eight hundred sound features, fifteen hundred short subjects, nineteen thousand still negatives, legal files, and press books, in addition to screenplays for the bulk of the Warner Brothers product from 1930 to 1950. For the purposes of this project, the company has granted the Center whatever publication rights it holds to the Warner films. In so doing, UA has provided the Center another opportunity to advance the cause of film scholarship.

Our goal in publishing these Warner Brothers screenplays is to explicate the art of screenwriting during the thirties and forties, the so-called Golden Age of Hollywood. In preparing a critical introduction and annotating the screenplay, the editor of each volume is asked to cover such topics as the development of the screenplay from its source to the final shooting script, differences between the final shooting script and the release print, production information, exploitation and critical reception of the film, its historical importance, its directorial style, and its position within the genre. He is also encouraged to go beyond these guidelines to incorporate supplemental information concerning the studio system of motion picture production.

We could set such an ambitious goal because of the richness of the script files in the Warner Film Library. For many film titles, the files might contain the property (novel, play, short story, or original story idea), research materials, variant drafts of scripts (from story outline to treatment to shooting script), post-production items such as press books and dialogue continuities, and legal records (details of the acquisition of the property, copyright registration, and contracts with actors and directors). Editors of the Wisconsin/Warner Bros. Screenplay Series receive copies of all the materials, along with prints of the films (the most authoritative ones available for reference purposes), to use in preparing the introductions and annotating the final shooting scripts.

In the process of preparing the screenplays for publication, typographical errors were corrected, punctuation and capitalization were modernized, and the format was redesigned to facilitate readability.

Unless otherwise specified, the photographs are frame enlargements taken from a 35-mm print of the film provided by United Artists.

In 1977 Warner Brothers donated the company's production records and distribution records to the University of Southern California and Princeton University, respectively. These materials are now available to researchers and complement the contents of the Warner Film Library donated to the Center by United Artists.

Tino Balio
General Editor

Acknowledgments

The following individuals were of considerable help to me in various ways: Albert Cavens, Brendan Carroll, Byron Haskin, Sally Hope, George Korngold, Miles Kreuger, Kathy McCormick, Phil Raskin, Carl Stucke, and the late Delmer Daves and Seton I. Miller.

I also wish to thank Robert Knutson and his extremely helpful staff in the Department of Special Collections, Doheny Library, University of Southern California.

R. B.

Introduction: *The Heroic Virtues*

Rudy Behlmer

The Sea Hawk—Captain Blood—Scaramouche. What images these names bring forth: high adventure, swashbuckling costume romance, derring-do, and bigger-than-life heroes.

The three novels about these colorful characters by Rafael Sabatini were surprise best sellers in the early 1920s. Sabatini had been writing historical romances in England since 1901, mostly for a small but enthusiastic group of admirers. For years he was turned down by American publishers. Then, with the appearance of *Scaramouche* (1921) Sabatini found himself an acclaimed commercial success. There was a scramble to republish in America many of his relatively obscure earlier works to cash in on the wave. Among these was his 1915 novel, *The Sea-Hawk*. It proved to be as popular as *Scaramouche* and *Captain Blood* (1922).

Hollywood responded to Sabatini's vogue and produced silent film versions of the three novels. After completing the sound remake of *Captain Blood* in 1935, Warner Brothers decided to follow that successful venture with another Sabatini sea story as a starring vehicle for the screen's newest swashbuckler, Errol Flynn. *The Sea Hawk* was the logical choice. By the time it was produced in 1940, tne Warner Brothers studio in Burbank was considered one of the smoothest-functioning operations of the major studios, and *The Sea Hawk* a superior example of the kind of big-budget action spectacle that Warners was second to none in producing. By dissecting *The Sea Hawk*'s step-by-step evolution, from Sabatini through the nine versions of the script by four writers, to the released film, a case history of collaborative film making on an exceptionally elaborate scale emerges. Impor-

11

tant creative talents in various areas contributed strongly to the realization of this project. Most were Warner Brothers employees—producers, writers, art directors, director, cameraman, special effects team, editor, composer-conductor—and each left a significant mark on the finished work, the melding of which still displayed the Warners house style. The antithesis of an auteur film, *The Sea Hawk* is the result of all the better aspects of the collaborative policy that was the foundation of the old studio system.

The Swashbuckling Tradition

Although the 1940 film has its origin in the 1915 Sabatini novel, Sabatini and his tale gradually were left behind as the various writers assigned to the film individually decided to emphasize characters and situations other than those present in the novel. But the spirit of Sabatini and the swashbuckling films of the 1920s—particularly those of Douglas Fairbanks—permeate the development of the production.

Sabatini was a disciple of the Alexandre Dumas school of romantic swashbuckling adventure of which *The Three Musketeers* (1844) and *The Count of Monte Cristo* (1844) were the prototype novels. He was also influenced by Mary Johnston (*To Have and to Hold*), one of the better writers of historical romances at the time. "The secret of her power," Sabatini said, "lies in the fact that her writings read as the chronicling not of things studied but of things remembered, of things personally witnessed."[1] Sabatini meticulously researched his chosen period. Then his inventive and convoluted incidents were bathed in a rich prose, which was carefully structured to complement his themes of injustice, revenge, and reconciliation. Escapist readers of the time delighted in every melodramatic page.

Along with Sabatini's literary limelight in the early 1920s, Douglas Fairbanks on the screen became even more popular than he had been previously when he made the decision to appear in a series of costume pieces that were tailored to his

1. Grant Overton, "Salute to Sabatini," *The Bookman*, February 1925, p. 730.

particular style. *The Mark of Zorro* (1920), *The Three Musketeers* (1921), *Robin Hood* (1922), and *The Black Pirate* (1926) were the prototypal and quintessential swashbucklers of the screen. Doug's basic down-to-earth screen character, aglow with an infectious blend of optimism, humor, and acrobatics, was superimposed over the more traditional historical romance and swashbuckling elements.

The most popular of the Sabatini silent screen adaptations was the First National production of *The Sea Hawk* in 1924, a faithful-to-the book and lavish spectacle starring Milton Sills. It grossed nearly two million dollars—big money in those days. Warner Brothers acquired rights to *The Sea Hawk* and *Captain Blood* (made by Vitagraph in 1924) after absorbing First National and Vitagraph in the late 1920s. Both properties were considered for remakes, but after sound and the Depression arrived, the swashbuckling genre went out of fashion. Instead the accent was on contemporary themes, situations, music, and dialogue.

A new era of pure swashbuckling costume films began when Warners decided to remake *Captain Blood*, following the popularity in 1934 of *The Count of Monte Cristo* (Reliance-United Artists) and *Treasure Island* (MGM)—each containing some aspects of the swashbuckling formula. Within the next five years fresh versions were produced of *The Three Musketeers* (RKO, 1935), *The Prisoner of Zenda* (Selznick-United Artists, 1937), *The Adventures of Robin Hood* (Warners, 1938), *The Buccaneer* (Paramount, 1938), *If I Were King* (Paramount, 1938), *The Man in the Iron Mask* (Small-United Artists, 1939), *The Son of Monte Cristo* (Small-United Artists, 1940), *The Mark of Zorro* (20th Century-Fox, 1940), and *The Sea Hawk* (Warners, 1940). All were filled with the ritualistic time-honored ingredients that proved to be perfect escapist fare for an audience coming out of the Depression and on the verge of World War II. Swashbucklers dealt with the heroic virtues. Usually there was an idealized hero defending the honor of a lady in a chivalrous and charming manner. Evil incarnate villains were to be dispatched, but in a "romantically violent," stylized series of action set-pieces that were usually rendered with less than graphic reality. Color, dash, romantic ardor, and excitement prevailed, and in the end, of course, there was the triumph of good over evil. Here was audience wish fulfillment on a grand scale.

Even before the 1935 *Captain Blood* was completed, Warners was convinced that *The Sea Hawk* would be a popular attraction. In renegotiating with Sabatini, the price of $25,000 was agreed upon to cover the "talking motion picture rights, including radio, television, novelizations not exceeding 5,000 words in length." (The price for the 1924 version had been $10,000.) Immediately writer Robert Neville was assigned to write a treatment of the novel.

Adapting the Story

Sabatini's fictitious tale dealt with Sir Oliver Tressilian, a Cornish gentleman of the sixteenth century, who is falsely accused of a murder actually committed by his half brother, Lionel. Lionel arranges to have Oliver kidnapped and carried away to sea. Oliver is taken prisoner and made a galley slave when the ship is attacked by a Spanish man-of-war and later, in turn, by Moors. The Moorish captain, Asad-ed-Din, Basha of Algiers, takes a liking to him and makes him his chief lieutenant. Soon Oliver's daring exploits are known on the seven seas. He is called Sakr-el-Bahr (the Hawk of the Sea).

Upon learning of the impending marriage of his English fiancée, Rosamund, to Lionel, the Sea Hawk heads his ship for England and kidnaps them both. But the Basha of Algiers desires Rosamund. The Sea Hawk fights him, and the ship's crew divides into two factions. After a bloody battle, the Sea Hawk wins. Then Lionel confesses to the murder of years ago, thereby clearing Oliver and allowing him to return to England with his beloved Rosamund.

Screenwriter Neville decided to make some drastic changes: he added a prologue involving Sir Francis Drake and the Spanish Armada, then introduced Queen Elizabeth and Lord Essex as major characters figuring prominently in the narrative. Another key character was invented: "La Tigra, a slender but sinewy girl in abbreviated pirate costume, a creature of savage beauty." All of this was interspersed with characters and ele-

14

ments from Sabatini's novel (including the galley scenes and escape), but the Sea Hawk's adventures did not include his becoming a follower of Mahmud, a Barbary corsair in full costume and "The Scourge of Christendom," as they did in the novel and the silent version.

Neither Elizabeth nor Essex was part of the original book and film. But Lytton Strachey's best-selling biography *Elizabeth and Essex* (1939), Maxwell Anderson's drama *Elizabeth the Queen* (1930), which had a long and prosperous run, and various other biographies and plays in the early 1930s dealing with Elizabeth may have influenced Neville—or one of the Warners executives—to include the popular characters in this version.

Neville's extended treatment is dated November 2, 1935. On December 14, Hal Wallis, Warners' executive producer, sent a memo to associate producer Harry Joe Brown, who had just completed *Captain Blood*, the film that would catapult Errol Flynn to stardom: "Will you please look over the material on *The Sea Hawk*, which we own, and let me know what you think of it as a possible follow-up on *Captain Blood* for a big sea picture on next year's program."[2]

Apparently Brown and Wallis were not sufficiently impressed with Neville's approach, and staff writer Delmer Daves was assigned to start all over. In his adaptation and screenplay, marked Temporary (April 17, 1936), Daves retained Elizabeth for a prologue only, during which the fictional Oliver Tressilian has distinguished himself in fighting the invincible Spanish Armada in association with the famed historical sea dog Sir John Hawkins. Daves may have been influenced by the reference in the novel to Tressilian's having commanded one of Queen Elizabeth's ships, which was responsible for dispersing the Spanish Armada. Daves has Elizabeth knight Tressilian in acknowledgment of his valor and gallant deeds at sea. The rest of the script adheres fairly close to Sabatini in general outline—including the Barbary corsair episodes.

Daves was not a great fan of the book. He wrote to me in 1968

2. This memo and all other correspondence quoted or referred to in the Introduction are from the Warner Brothers files in the Department of Special Collections, Doheny Library, University of Southern California.

that "the draft was only exploratory. . . . The book by Sabatini
was so florid and unbelievable I wrote an article for the annual
Variety or *The [Hollywood] Reporter* [the trade press] at their request re: the problems of adaptations to the screen in answer to
various critical protests over films 'violating' original materials,
books, plays, etc. The article was based on actual quotes from
the more extravagant and flowery scenes from the book which
would have turned the so-called drama into a farce."

It must be admitted that Daves had a point. The following is
an example of dialogue between Sir Oliver and his beloved
Rosamund near the conclusion of the novel:

He set his hands upon her shoulders, and held her so at arm's length
from him considering her with very tender eyes.

"Sweet lady!" he murmured, and sighed heavily. "God! How happy
might we not have been but for that evil chance . . ." He checked
abruptly. His hands fell from her shoulders to his sides, he half-turned
away, brusque now in tone and manner. "I grow maudlin. Your sweet
pity has so softened me that I had almost spoke of love; and what have I
to do with that? Love belongs to life; love is life; whilst I . . . *Moriturus
te salutat!*"

"Ah, no, no!" She was clinging to him again with shaking hands, her
eyes wild.

"It is too late," he answered her. "There is no bridge can span the pit
I have dug myself. I must go down into it as cheerfully as God will let
me."

"Then," she cried in sudden exaltation, "I will go with you. At the
last, at least, we shall be together." . . .

He started from her. "Hark! What's that?"

From without had come a sudden cry, "Afoot! To arms! To arms!"[3]

The author was clearly at his best with plot machinations,
period detail, and vividly described action scenes. As Brad Dar-
rach has stated, "Sabatini's heroes . . . all suffer from a terminal
case of pedestalism. They can stand up to any man alive . . .
but one glance at the heroine's chill charms throws them into
hilarious spasms of unworthiness."[4]

3. Rafael Sabatini, *The Sea-Hawk* (Boston and New York: Houghton Mifflin,
n.d.), pp. 316–17.
    4. *Time*, August 9, 1976, p. 71.

A few months elapsed after Daves finished his draft, and on September 10, 1936, Harry Joe Brown wrote Wallis:

After seeing *Last of the Mohicans* [Reliance-United Artists, 1936], then *Charge of the Light Brigade* [Warners, 1936] and other pictures that look like big money-getters, and are, I bring to your attention again *The Sea Hawk*. This has a more dramatic story than of the above mentioned pictures and even more action, if such a thing is possible. Surely enough time will have lapsed since *Captain Blood*, and anyway they are two entirely different stories, except for one situation [presumably the slave auction].

As a reminder: if you will recall, Hal, I wrote you that we have some marvelous battle scenes from the old picture [the silent *Sea Hawk*]. Here's hoping we go to work on it.

After seeing *Light Brigade*, I was very happy to see the great improvement in Flynn's work. He looked great to me in the picture, and he certainly should be "tops" of all his type.

Instead of proceeding with production plans for *The Sea Hawk*, Warners executives decided to move ahead with another big-budget Flynn film, *The Adventures of Robin Hood* (1938). In early 1938, Seton I. Miller, who had been the co-writer on *Robin Hood*, was given the *Sea Hawk* material to see what his approach would be. Miller had entered motion pictures playing a small role in *Brown of Harvard* (1926). His screenwriting credits include *The Criminal Code, Scarface, The Last Mile, The Dawn Patrol, G-Men,* and *Kid Galahad*. By now Henry Blanke (*Robin Hood*) had been assigned as associate producer of *The Sea Hawk*.[5] On August 25 Miller submitted a twenty-five-page outline to Blanke called "Beggars of the Sea." It had nothing whatsoever to do with Sabatini's *Sea-Hawk*. Instead, Miller took a hint from the inclusion of Queen Elizabeth and the Spanish Armada from Neville and Daves and devised an entirely new approach and plot, which went this way:

King Philip II of Spain, through his ambassador, is using diplomatic pressure on Elizabeth to prevent England from building a navy by demanding that she halt her English pirates from

5. The term "associate producer" in 1940 was changed from "supervisor" in the early 1930s and then became "producer" in 1942. The function was that of a staff "line producer" in most cases.

further depredations on Spanish treasure ships. Backed by the lord admiral and the "sea beggars," Captain Geoffrey Thorpe suspects King Philip's plans but cannot entirely convince the queen. However, he plays on her cupidity and dislike of Philip in a way to secure her permission for a daring raid on the Spanish treasure train in Panama—with the understanding that his diversion of resources will enable England to build a sorely needed fleet.

By a series of intrigues and devices the Spanish ambassador and the traitorous lord treasurer discover Thorpe's intentions and set a trap for him in Panama. After he is captured and sentenced to the galley, Thorpe learns from Spanish officers that the armies of the Spanish Duke of Alva and the Duke of Norfolk are now ready to move against a defenseless England in order to put Mary Queen of Scots on the throne. This motivates a desperate coup on the part of the English prisoners, who seize and make off with the Spanish boat and return to England in time to warn the queen of her danger.

Upon reading the information in the documents that Thorpe brings, Elizabeth abandons her policy of trying to maintain friendly relations with Spain, frees the "sea beggars," and makes ready to defend her country and gain its naval supremacy by building the fleet which the "sea beggars" have always had as their goal.

Miller outlined two possible conclusions: One, a "spectacle finish," has Thorpe and the "beggars of the sea" participating in the destruction of Philip's fleet at Cadiz. The other "intimate finish" depicts the queen finally realizing the strength and loyalty of the "beggars" and commissioning Thorpe and the others to raid Cadiz in the near future.

The historical backdrop used by Miller was, on the whole, reasonably accurate. Captain Thorpe was loosely based on Sir Francis Drake, the famous British sea captain who was the first Englishman to circumnavigate the world (1577–80) and later was vice admiral of the British fleet that defeated the Armada. But curiously, the "sea beggars" of history were what *Dutch* privateers of the time were called; their English equivalents were referred to as "sea dogs" (Drake, Hawkins, Frobisher, etc.)

Blanke apparently was enthusiastic about Miller's work. On September 6 he wrote to Wallis: "I am sending you . . . *Beggars of the Sea*, which you may have known under the title of *Sea Hawk*. . . . I think it offers twice the possibilities of a *Captain Blood* and will make a sequel to *Robin Hood*." Then Miller was told to develop his outline into a script, which he completed in late 1938. Nothing of consequence was changed; the material merely was expanded.

Shortly afterward Wallis decided to postpone work on *The Sea Hawk* (or "Beggars of the Sea") for the time being. Instead, Flynn and Bette Davis were cast in an expensive Technicolor version of Maxwell Anderson's play *Elizabeth the Queen* (release title: *The Private Lives of Elizabeth and Essex*, 1938). This property had been purchased specifically for Davis in 1938.

In the meantime, Miller went to work on *Dust Be My Destiny* (1939) with the promise that when "Beggars of the Sea" was reactivated he would be put back on it. But Milton Krims, another Warners staff writer, was given the assignment in early March 1939. Miller wrote to Wallis, on March 15:

> Considering that I took *The Sea Hawk*, an out-dated piece of junk, and wrote an entirely original screenplay that Henry [Blanke] was most enthusiastic about and [director] Mike Curtiz even more so, I think I at least deserve to follow through and make what revisions they want on it. If I failed to accomplish the revisions they wanted, then I would think another writer should take it over.
>
> Secondly, I believe I can accomplish the work in a much shorter time, as Milton—in order to do justice to the history, period, and characters of the story—will have to cover all the research again whereas I can pick it up at this point and go on.
>
> I put my guts into this original and would like to have the opportunity of seeing it through to a final draft.

Miller completed another draft on May 13, 1939. There were no major changes in narrative or dialogue, but an opening scene in the council chamber of Philip II was added. Then, on the recommendation of Warners staff writer (soon to be director) John Huston, Henry Blanke sent writer Howard Koch the latest script on "Beggars of the Sea." Koch recently had been put under contract, shortly after the sensational response to the

Orson Welles 1938 radio broadcast of *War of the Worlds*, which he had adapted from the H. G. Wells novella. His friend Huston,[6] along with Koch's part in the Martian episode, had been responsible for Warners' hiring Koch.

On the basis of the Miller script, the budget was now estimated at $1,400,000. On July 5 Blanke reported by letter to vacationing Wallis that after several budget meetings the most that could be cut from this figure was $50,000. Blanke did not want to authorize any rewriting that would eliminate or cut down the action sequences, "as this is the main point we have to sell."

After Wallis returned, he sent a memo to Blanke on July 24 in which he laid out changes that he and director Michael Curtiz had discussed. There had been some scenes that took place at Dover, following the first sea battle; scenes both before and after Thorpe's audience with the queen, which led into a fight in a tavern; and an eavesdropping episode wherein the lord treasurer's spy learns that Thorpe is going to Panama. These scenes and this method of discovery were eliminated, making it possible to cut down on some sets. It was agreed that all references to the beggars of the sea were to be dropped; instead, the privateers would be called "sea hawks."[7] Wallis and Curtiz also decided, in Wallis's words, "to use [footage from] practically all of the fight on the two ships from [the 1935] *Captain Blood*, which will mean a tremendous saving as Mike agrees that he could not shoot a better fight today than he made at the time in *Captain Blood.* . . . From Panama on I don't think there will be many changes in the construction." By now the budget was down to $1,161,000.

Howard Koch's Screenplay

After reading Miller's material and attending the various meetings, Koch drafted a thirty-eight-page "suggested story treat-

6. In Koch's *The Lonely Man* (produced in May 1937 by the Federal Theatre at the Blackstone Theatre in Chicago) Huston had played Abraham Lincoln, reincarnated as a liberal professor in a small college and a lawyer for labor unions.

7. *The Sea Hawk* was considered a salable, sure-fire title. The silent picture had been a success, of course, and other similar film titles abounded: *The Sea Bat, The Sea Beast, The Sea Lion, The Sea Panther, The Sea Tiger,* and several versions of *The Sea Wolf.*

ment," which essentially was the same story Miller had written, with the same sequences, for the most part, and the same characters. Koch has Thorpe, after delivering the implicating dispatches to the queen, at sea with the historical Lord Howard, the lord high admiral of England, discussing tactics to be used in confronting the Armada. Then Koch included the actual battle (with Thorpe and Lord Howard), ending with the Spanish caught between the damaging fire of the English and the gathering fury of a storm. The crippled Armada, with no friendly harbor in reach, was not in condition to face a gale in the unfamiliar and treacherous waters of the Northern Channel. The Spanish fleet retreated and was dispersed by the storm. In his treatment Koch says:

> In this climactic incident we cap our theme that, in the struggle for supremacy between England and Spain, the gods favored the people who put their trust in the winds against those who depended on the oars of slaves. Fortunately, history happens to bear out this thesis in the actual manner by which the Armada's destruction was accomplished.

Koch began his treatment with this note:

> Since the source of *The Sea Hawk* is obviously the exploits of Sir Francis Drake, it is suggested that an introductory acknowledgement be made to the effect that the leading character is based upon Drake, without adhering to an exact, factual record. This would lend more interest to the narrative, and, at the same time, justify the historical parallels evident to anyone familiar with the history of that period.

The treatment was followed by a Final screenplay, written by Koch, dated August 28 to September 21, 1939. The Armada finale was eliminated at this point. In a letter to Walter Mac-Ewen, executive story editor, Miller described accurately the similarities and differences between his script and Koch's. This was instigated by a writing credit dispute that came up in early 1940. Miller says in a letter dated March 18, 1940:

> I can't understand upon what basis Mr. Koch claims sole [screenplay] credit on *Sea Hawk*. . . .
> The characters and characterizations are the same from the heroes to heavies . . . except for the shading on Elizabeth, who is not played with my bellicoseness, and Alvarez [the Spanish ambassador] and

Wolfingham [the traitorous English lord] being more mild and diplomatic. And Maria's Spanish servant has become an English companion. The inter-relationship between the characters is the same.

Koch has introduced new business, such as the [navigation] charts [which, combined with the court astronomer's interpretation of same, reveals Thorpe's destination] and [Thorpe's pet] monkey, but has retained the major portion of mine.

The story and plot are exactly the same except that Koch uses the threat of the Armada against England instead of Alva's land army [and the Duke of Norfolk's]. . . .

In the process of shortening and tightening he dropped some sequences, replaced a few and added the chartmaker routines. His most important sequence reconstruction was sinking the first Spanish boat, having Thorpe take Maria aboard his own and was thereby able to get the romance much further advanced in the early part of the script and to have a few more scenes between Thorpe and Maria. A swell asset. Koch effectively built up a lot of the scenes in his redialoguing, but many of the lines carry the same connotation and many were retained from my script with little or no re-wording. . . .

To me the fair credit would be Original Story by Miller, Screen Play by Koch and Miller (story suggested by the Sabatini title or novel). I regret losing the Original credit but can understand the sales value the studio places on the Sabatini name. . . .

P.S. Although I based Thorpe's character on Drake, Hawkins and Frobisher, I believe it is a mistake to openly identify Thorpe with Drake in a sub-title. The raid on Panama is from Drake, but otherwise Thorpe's adventures vary so widely from Drake's history that the British may resent taking large dramatic liberties with their naval hero, where they wouldn't with a presumably fictitious character.

Koch's rebuttal was put forth in a letter to MacEwen dated March 20:

What I feel Miller fails to realize is that a situation may look similar because of its place, order and participating characters, but at the same time be so vastly different in its motivations and dramatic content as to constitute a change in plot.

Actually, Miller's conflict is with Sabatini and not with me, since Sabatini is getting credit which has no basis in fact—credit for original material that I believe Miller should have.

Judging from his letter it seems that he misunderstood my attitude. I have not wanted him to lose credit for the material he furnished. If he can't get this credit on the actual basis of original material, I have already offered to share in the credit for the screenplay. At the same time, I feel it would be entirely unreasonable to ask me to give up *first* screen credit in order to compensate him for his concession to Sabatini.

All along, Wallis wanted to retain Rafael Sabatini's name in conjunction with the screen credits and advertising and publicity for *The Sea Hawk*. He believed that Sabatini carried a certain draw, and that his name was synonymous with costume adventure and more specifically with sea adventure (by 1940 three different volumes dealing with Captain Blood and one titled *The Black Swan* had been published). From a contractual standpoint, regardless of how much Warners departed from Sabatini's novel, the studio still had the right to use the title *The Sea Hawk* but needed Sabatini's permission to use his name in connection with any specific film. He refused after reading the script, objecting that the film story was too great a departure from his novel. When the picture was given an international reissue in 1947, however, Sabatini's name got into the advertising matter through an inadvertence in the studio's publicity department. Sabatini, through his attorney, reasserted his original claim. Then Warners, for an agreed-upon sum, arranged for the use of Sabatini's name in all then-current and future distribution of the film.

In examining the various drafts, it is clear that the primary difference between Miller's scripts and Koch's scripts is in the dialogue, characterization, and interplay. Koch did rewrite a good many of the scenes in a different style; and he gave more dimension to the basically stereotyped characters. A typical example is a scene between Queen Elizabeth and Captain Thorpe (figure 13), written by Miller for his last draft, the Revised Temporary script dated May 13, 1939. The scene is reproduced in the Appendix and should be compared with Koch's reworking of the same material on pages 104–11 of this volume and with the film. Clearly, Koch has used the same situation, but the differences are in the relationship of the characters, the relative subtlety, the building up of the scene, the humor, and the literate dialogue.

Basically, Koch's script—and Miller's earlier versions, for that

23

matter—are well-constructed five-act plays. Standard swashbuckling ingredients are carefully included along the way. There is little repetition of incident; we are allowed one sea battle, one land battle, one capture, one escape, one major duel (to the death), and one romance with assorted "love" scenes. Formula elements from *Captain Blood* and *The Adventures of Robin Hood* were interwoven for box-office insurance. The pirate/outlaw status of the hero is presented as justifiable and motivated by injustice, tyranny, and patriotism, thereby making his position respectable. The heroine is at first ignorant of what the hero is trying to do in his cause and dislikes him for his superficial pirate/outlaw status, then gradually learns to understand and support him, and at last, with a reconciliation scene, to love him fervently. This is all accomplished in approximately three "love" scenes—each reflecting an advanced case of the hero and heroine's involvement with each other (figures 8, 9, and 10). Act One ends when the crew of Thorpe's ship sights Dover following the first battle; Act Two concludes with Thorpe's sailing from Dover while Maria stands on the dock; Act Three takes us up to the capture of Thorpe and his men after the aborted treasure train episode in Panama; Act Four ends following the escape from the galley. Climaxes are properly spaced, and suspense mounts in direct ratio to the progression of each act.

As the preparation of the film continued, Henry Blanke began to worry about two British films made in the mid-1930s that he vaguely recalled as having covered some of the same ground as *The Sea Hawk*. *Drake of England* (1935)—released in the United States on a very limited basis as *Drake the Pirate*—was a filmed version of *Drake*, Louis N. Parker's play of 1912. It telescoped some of the highlights of the Elizabethan sea dog's adventuresome career, including his attack on a Spanish treasure train on the Isthmus of Panama. This attack was the basis for a lengthy sequence in the 1940 version of *The Sea Hawk* and in the 1935 version of *Drake of England*. Historically, such an attack was committed only by Drake and by no one else. Both *The Sea Hawk* and *Drake of England* inaccurately portrayed Drake (Thorpe) meeting the queen before his expedition to Panama and the queen giving her tacit consent to this trip. In fact, Drake was not introduced to Queen Elizabeth until *after* his return. However, the queen secretly connived with Drake before he left on his famous voyage around the world in which she actually had an interest.

While the material in the play and film version of Parker's *Drake* is based, to a large degree, on fact, most of the occurrences in *The Sea Hawk* are entirely fictitious: the attack on the Spanish ambassador's ship, the entire love story, the capture of Thorpe (Drake) near the Isthmus of Panama, his condemnation to be a galley slave, and his final escape from the galley with the plans for the Armada. Historically no major British captain was ever captured by the Spaniards.

Alexander Korda's *Fire over England* (1936), the other British film that Blanke remembered as having some parallels with *The Sea Hawk*, was a much more lavish and prestigious production than *Drake of England*. Loosely based on the novel by A.E.W. Mason, the film dealt fictitiously with a young friend (Laurence Olivier) of Queen Elizabeth (Flora Robson) who goes in disguise to the court of Philip II (Raymond Massey) to find out the names of British subjects in Spanish pay. Successful, he returns to England, is knighted, and then helps to defeat Philip's great Armada. The "love interest" was supplied by Vivien Leigh. Obviously the two stories are quite different. But some aspects presented similarities, for example, the scenes in which the Spanish ambassador appears before the queen protesting the activities of the English pirates against Spain. In both films, the ambassador threatens with war, whereupon the queen retaliates with anger. This is historically accurate.

After a lengthy examination of both *Fire over England* and *Drake of England* by Warners' legal staff, it was determined that any similarities to *The Sea Hawk* were due to the same background and basis in historical facts.

Preproduction

In the summer of 1939, *The Private Lives of Elizabeth and Essex* finished filming. The plan was to begin work shortly thereafter on *The Sea Hawk*. In fact, on April 5, Wallis had written Tenny

Wright, the studio production manager: "In planning your sets for *The Knight and the Lady* [*The Private Lives of Elizabeth and Essex*], please plan these on stages where they can be saved after this production as we will be able to use practically every set over again for *The Sea Hawk* and this will save a fortune."

But various circumstances caused *The Sea Hawk* to be postponed again for six months. Flynn objected strenuously to the idea of following one long and difficult-to-shoot costume epic with an even more lengthy and arduous production. Another Flynn vehicle, *Dodge City*, released in April of 1939, was an enormous hit with the public, and Warners decided to rush into production a follow-up to be called *Virginia City* (1940). Most important, postponing *The Sea Hawk* allowed sufficient time for the planning and construction of a unique new "maritime" sound stage on the Warners' Burbank lot. After its completion, Stage 21 (at the time the largest and most modern in the film industry) was capable of being filled with water. Thousands of feet of heavy mains, sewers, and drains had been installed. Working in several shifts daily, 375 men were employed for eleven weeks in the construction of a full-scale British man-of-war (135 feet) and a Spanish galleass (165 feet), which were placed side by side, with some distance separating them, in the water on the stage. A pit between the two ships reached down several feet below stage level, making it possible for stunt men to fall into the water from the decks. Around the pit the "ocean" had a depth of only a few feet.

The ships were erected on steel platforms that, in turn, were mounted on wheels that worked on a series of tracks. Hydraulic jacks could rock the vessels from side to side. Previously, no ship the size of these had been built especially for stage work, either indoors or outdoors.

Surrounding the two ships, a huge painted muslin cyclorama served as both sea and sky. Art director Anton Grot developed a ripple machine, as it was called, that created the illusion of moving ocean water—from normal waves to rough seas—by sliding sheets of "wave silhouettes" up and down in front of lights behind the ocean-painted cyclorama. (The ship scenes for the 1935 *Captain Blood* also had been shot on a Warners sound stage, but only portions of the ships were used at one time. There were not the flooded stage, tracks, rockers, and so on.)

Warner Brothers did not believe in building practical ships and filming at sea—as, for example, MGM did for *Mutiny on the Bounty* (1935). Too often in such enterprises there were weather delays, seasickness, temperamental outbursts, and other grief that could cost considerable time and money. This marine stage, which no other studio had, allowed for filming sea pictures under totally controlled conditions. The studio planned to film *The Sea Wolf, Captain Horatio Hornblower*, and *John Paul Jones* on the stage in the immediate future, but only the first of these was completed. After America entered World War II the studio suspended plans for expensive period nautical films.[8] (Stage 21 was destroyed by fire in May 1952.)

Starting in November, the casting of *The Sea Hawk* was given serious attention. Flynn, of course, was always figured for the lead since the picture was designed at the outset as a vehicle for him. But back in July, Wallis wrote to Curtiz: "I want to make a complete and thorough test of Dennis Morgan in the character of the leading role for *The Sea Hawk*. . . . You will have Brenda Marshall or Jane Bryan work with him in the girl's scenes. . . ." Morgan, whose background was primarily as a singer, recently had been signed by the studio. Wallis's request was no doubt the result of one of the many recurring battles between Flynn and Jack L. Warner that centered on the kind of picture the studio wanted the actor to do, the chosen director (he disliked Curtiz intensely but was often directed by him), and his approval of leading ladies. In any case, nothing was changed after testing Dennis Morgan; Flynn was still scheduled for the temporarily delayed *Sea Hawk*. Although originally announced for *The Sea Hawk*, Olivia de Havilland, his popular costar from *Captain Blood, The Charge of the Light Brigade, The Adventures of Robin Hood*, and other films, was not cast. Neither Flynn nor de Havilland wanted to go on working together. After her loan-out to

8. Much later both *Captain Horatio Hornblower* (1951) and *John Paul Jones* (1959), in addition to Warners' *The Crimson Pirate* (1952), *The Master of Ballantrae* (1953), and *Moby Dick* (1956), were all photographed using regular ships on the seas of Europe.

Selznick for the role of Melanie in *Gone with the Wind* (1939), she returned to Warners determined to seek better parts at her home studio—and this included not wanting to continue as "the girl" in the Flynn adventure films. Jack L. Warner was equally determined to keep Olivia in her place by showing the actress that her presence in *Gone with the Wind* neither impressed him nor changed her status at Warners.

Instead, Brenda Marshall was cast (figures 7 and 9). Following a brief appearance on Broadway in 1938, she had signed as a contract player and was being given a buildup. In her first film at the studio, *Espionage Agent* (1939), she had the leading female role. *The Sea Hawk* was her second film. Others in consideration included Andrea Leeds, Margaret Lockwood, Jane Bryan, Ida Lupino, and Geraldine Fitzgerald.

For the important role of the queen the studio wanted Flora Robson (figure 12), the distinguished British actress of stage and screen who had played Elizabeth in Korda's *Fire over England*. Warners signed her to come to America on a two-picture deal, the first to be an important leading role in *We Are Not Alone* (1939) with Paul Muni and Jane Bryan, and the second to be *The Sea Hawk*. When *The Sea Hawk* was delayed she agreed to transfer the commitment to *Invisible Stripes* (1940) with George Raft and to add *The Sea Hawk* as a third film if and when that project was reactivated. Other players considered for Queen Elizabeth included Judith Anderson, Gale Sondergaard, and Geraldine Fitzgerald.

Claude Rains, under nonexclusive contract to Warners, always had been first choice for Don Alvarez, the Spanish ambassador (figures 7 and 16). Basil Rathbone was originally favored as his cohort in villainy, Lord Wolfingham, which would have reprised the duo from *Robin Hood*. But instead Henry Daniell, the number two choice, was signed (figure 16). Others on the list of possibilities for Wolfingham were Vincent Price, George Sanders, and Louis Hayward. Alan Hale, as usual, was cast as Flynn's sidekick, and Una O'Connor virtually reprised her role in *Robin Hood* as the heroine's companion.

Production

The last few weeks before filming began saw a flurry of activity all over the Warners lot. *The Sea Hawk* had an exceptionally big budget and complex logistics. Because its production is a particularly interesting example of the unique mesh of procedures then current, a relatively detailed account of the making of the film follows. By the late 1930s the Warner Studio in Burbank was an extremely well-oiled and smoothly integrated machine that was equipped with up-to-the-minute facilities and technical virtuosity. In the case of this major enterprise every department was called upon to outdo itself.

The Sea Hawk can be regarded as the high-water mark of epics made on a studio lot. Only a few years later, such a film automatically would be shot, at least in part, on location. Almost nothing in *The Sea Hawk* was shot outside of the Burbank lot—except for a short sequence representing Venta Cruz (in Panama) photographed at the Warner ranch at Calabasas, and a brief beach scene photographed at nearby Point Magu. Everything else—Philip's palace in Spain, the sea battle in the English Channel, Queen Elizabeth's court (figures 11 and 20), the Panama jungles (figures 17 and 18), the Spanish galleys (figure 21), the coast of Seville, Dover, and more—was concocted entirely within the confines of the studio.

The Sea Hawk was given a forty-eight-day shooting schedule. Because of Flora Robson's commitment for the Broadway production of *Ladies in Retirement*, her scenes had to be shot first. They involved many supporting players who appeared only in the sequences in the palace. These were filmed on Stage 7 where the *Elizabeth and Essex* throne room had been photographed. Art director Anton Grot, who had designed the settings for that picture, artfully modified them for *The Sea Hawk*, and some of the set units as well as set decorations were reused according to plan.

Queen Elizabeth's palace interiors as rendered are not to be taken as realistic, detailed reproductions of any of the royal palaces of her time. Grot's sets were seemingly enormous, with high ceilings and glossy dark floors. In 1936 Grot said, "I for one, do not like extremely realistic sets. . . . There is a difference between creating an impression and becoming impressionistic. . . . If the sets should happen to be too realistic it would detract from the action and the beautiful costumes."[9]

Orry-Kelly designed the costumes for both *Elizabeth and Essex* and *The Sea Hawk* and was able to revamp some of his earlier creations in addition to planning new costumes for some of the principal players.

On February 1, 1940, filming began. Curtiz's favorite cameraman, Sol Polito, was shooting in black and white. Warners did not make a film in the Technicolor process for twenty-one months during the period between *Elizabeth and Essex* and *Dive Bomber* (1941). Although few Technicolor films were produced at any studio in the late 1930s and early 1940s, this was an unusual period of curtailment. Since the plan all along for *The Sea Hawk* was to use a considerable amount of stock footage from black and white films, that may have been the reason for foregoing Technicolor in this case. Fortunately, Polito's photography is a superb example of how extraordinary black and white can be.

Once filming had begun, Wallis, as was his custom, fired off volleys of memos to Curtiz, Tenny Wright, Henry Blanke, and various others involved in the realization of the film. He seemingly was on top of everything that was going on with regard to production. After viewing the first two days' dailies, Wallis started in on Curtiz:

> I noticed in the scene with Flynn where the monkey jumps on his arm that you are starting to ad lib the script again. The added lines about a lot of monkeys already living in the palace and the pulling the tail line are ad lib cracks put in on the set and have a tendency to make the scene phoney because they are colloquialisms and take the whole thing out of character. I don't want to have a lot of trouble with you on this picture and at the same time wear myself out, but here you are the second day of the picture, after religiously promising me that you would let the script alone, already putting in ad lib cracks which do nothing but hurt the scenes.

9. Donald Deschner, "Anton Grot," *The Velvet Light Trap*, no. 15 (Fall 1975), p. 22.

What are you going to do about this? Are you going to keep harassing me all through this picture or are you going to shoot the script?

Two days later Wallis wrote to Blanke:

I wish Flynn had referred to Robson at least two or three times in the dialogue as "Your Majesty" or "Your Highness," as it was written in the script, instead of calling her Madam all of the time. It gets a little monotonous, and at the same time it seems to lack the dignity and respect. . . . Why was this changed? Why don't they quit messing around with the scenes and let the stuff alone? . . . The effect that we were trying to get with a dashing soldier talking to his Queen is lost. It sounds instead like somebody having a conversation with the owner of a hook shop.

Despite Wallis's complaints, the above material remained in the film.[10] It is likely that Howard Koch changed some of the dialogue. In his American Film Institute Oral History, Koch recalls spending time on the set of *The Sea Hawk:*

At the time, I really didn't know that writers were supposed, when they finished a script, to disappear and get on another assignment and not bother their producer and director and actors. He could appear on the set the first day; but I kept coming down to see whether the director was getting on the screen what I had envisioned. For a while, Mike Curtiz appreciated this, because he saw that I was really interested. When he needed a line, I was there to give it, and so on. But when I began to criticize certain things, Mike was not so interested in my being on the set. Finally, he sent a memo to the front office asking that I be kept off the set. I came down on the set one day and there was a guard at the door telling me I couldn't get in. Through the intercession of Flynn, I used to go around the back way and I got in anyway. I kept fighting with Mike, and I would go through Flynn, who backed me pretty much and who, by the way, I liked very much. Flynn, with all the stories about him . . . I found to be a very honest man who didn't pull the star business. In fact, he made fun of it.

Dame Flora Robson recently recalled working with Flynn on *The Sea Hawk*. They both felt that a man like Thorpe would treat the queen in some ways like another man and not be too deferential toward her. Of Flynn she said:

10. In Parker's play *Drake*, Queen Elizabeth is consistently addressed as Madam by members of her court and Drake.

We hit it off from the beginning. He was naughty about his homework. I told him that because he couldn't remember his lines it would hold up the picture and I would be delayed going to New York to do a play. When I told him this, he was very kind and learned his lines to help me: the work went so fast we were finished by four in the afternoon on some days. I remember Mike Curtiz saying to him, "What's the matter with you? You know all your words."[11]

The first month was taken up primarily with scenes in the palace in order to finish many of the featured players who did not appear in other settings. Claude Rains's scenes on the Spanish ship and on Thorpe's ship were done next so that this expensive actor would not be on the payroll too long.

By February 19, the climactic duel between Flynn and Henry Daniell was being filmed before finishing with the palace sets (figure 24). Unit manager Frank Mattison in his report to Tenny Wright said:

This duel has turned into a matter of a walk. Mr. Daniell is absolutely helpless and his closeups in the duel will be mostly from the elbows up.

Mr. Curtiz was greatly discouraged with his results on Saturday, as well as Friday, but there is nothing we can do as it will be impossible to go back and change to someone else in this part [since so many scenes with Daniell already had been filmed].

The Casting Office and everyone connected with the picture were duly warned of Mr. Daniell's inability to fence long before the picture started, and we knew of him being taken out of a part in *Romeo & Juliet* [MGM, 1936] because he could not handle a sword.

By March 1 the company was six days behind schedule because both Flynn and Curtiz had been home ill for several days and Daniell was unable to perform the stage fencing. "The man tries hard but it has just taken about four extra days to get through this duel," said Mattison on March 1.

The duel—an obligatory scene in the Flynn swashbucklers—was choreographed by Belgian fencing master Fred Cavens, who had staged some of Douglas Fairbanks's duels in the 1920s. Working with Curtiz, Cavens devised a routine that took Flynn

11. Charles Higham, *Errol Flynn: The Untold Story* (Garden City, N.Y.: Doubleday, 1980), p. 128.

(doubled in some shots by Don Turner) and Daniell (doubled in most shots by Ralph Faulkner and Ned Davenport) from Wolfingham's sitting room in the palace to balcony, corridor, and main hall. The fight was more furiously paced and edited than the Cavens duels for *Captain Blood* and *Robin Hood* (partly because of the necessity to double Daniell extensively). Overturned tables and candelabra stands, slashed candles, and huge shadows of the opponents on the wall were used much as they had been in *Robin Hood* (figure 24).

By mid-March the spectacular battle scene that took place near the opening of the film between Thorpe's ship and the Spanish galleass was being shot on the marine stage. Blanke sent a memo to Wallis on March 14 in which he outlined the footage he could lift from the 1935 *Captain Blood*: shots of men swinging from ship to ship during the battle, close-ups of cannons firing, and clips showing the effect of the cannons on the ship. In addition, he had some medium and long shots of general battle and men falling into the water (figure 5) originally used in *The Divine Lady* (1929), a rather lavish First National picture about Lord Nelson and Lady Hamilton, which had been reused in the 1935 *Captain Blood*. The fact that there was a discrepancy of roughly two centuries between the period of *The Sea Hawk* and *The Divine Lady* seemed to bother no one.

On March 14 Wallis wrote Tenny Wright:

For the past few days, I have been getting a lot of reports via the grapevine about Errol Flynn. Also, Mike has told me he loses hours every day on account of Flynn and is days behind because of him, that he doesn't know his lines, etc.

I also understand that Flynn is late on the set practically every day. . . . Do you know about these things? . . . and if you do, why don't you do something about it? If you can't do anything about it, why don't you at least let me in on it so that I can?

Filming on the sea battle continued. Wallis to Curtiz on March 19:

The long shots for the big crowd [on the ships], yesterday's dailies, were on the whole very good. There are some very effective shots. . . .
There are two or three things which I want to comment on, however.

33

. . . I noticed when the sailors cheer for any reason, that a great many of them use a clenched fist in what is really the Communist salute. This is very noticeable, and I don't understand why you allow the people to do it. . . .

The principal thing that bothered me was the mass of people, that thick, milling mass that prevented you from getting any action into the scene and those fakey wooden swords waving around in the air in front of the camera. Please do your best to get more effective action in your closer shots so that we can cut away from the fakey stuff. Somehow or other, the extras in these sets didn't seem to work very well. The swinging from one ship to another—they were hesitant, they fell all over themselves, stumbled over the rails, and it didn't have the swift, adventuresome feeling that it should have had. They looked like a lot of old men who were scared to death of what they were doing.

I don't mean to be so critical, Mike, but I know that you would want me to be, as there can be no fault found when striving for perfection, which is what we all want.

As I said at the beginning, the long shots themselves, the [camera] set-ups and all, the boats coming together, are very effective, and I am sure that we can get as much film out of the stuff as we will need to make the sequence effective.

After the battle between the two ships, all of the galley material was photographed on Stage 3 (figure 21). Scenes taking place in a galley with slaves shackled and rowing to the beat of the timekeeper's drum were relatively novel in 1940. Both the silent *Sea Hawk* and *Ben-Hur* (1925) had key episodes during which the hero spent time at the dreaded oars (picturizing, in both cases, chapters from the respective popular novels), but these had been years earlier and without dialogue.[12] *Les Miserables* (1935) had some galley material (as in the Hugo novel), but it was not expanded or developed in the manner of the early *Sea Hawk* and *Ben-Hur*.

Wallis was concerned about the amount of whipping of the rower-slaves being photographed. "As you know," Wallis wrote Curtiz, "we have been cautioned by the Hays Office against too much brutality, and the way you have been shooting

12. The *New York Times* reviewer of the 1924 *Sea Hawk* said, "We doubt if anybody who sees the scenes of the galley slaves will forget them. They are utterly different from any others presented in a film" (June 3, 1924).

34

the stuff, we won't be able to cut it out. You have far too much of it, and it's going to become offensive and repulsive." Apropos of this, at the time *Captain Blood* was being made in 1935 Robert Lord, a Warners associate producer, wrote Wallis asking, "Why do you have so much flogging, torturing and physical cruelty in *Captain Blood*? Does Mike [Curtiz] like it or do you think audiences will like it? Women and children will be warned to stay away from the picture—and justly so." Flynn was unhappy about the methods Curtiz used to gain "realism." He was particularly upset about the whipping scenes. Olivia de Havilland, who had worked on many films with Curtiz, has said that the director "was dynamic but an extremely tense man. He cared about his films, but not for the actors. Very difficult for me to adapt to, I must say. He was so abrasive and so hostile toward actors, especially towards Flynn." [13]

One of the exceptionally well-directed scenes in the picture was filmed next: Thorpe and his men freeing themselves from the galley. After a detailed escape from the shackles and chains (figure 22), the men cautiously begin their operation on the deck of the Spanish ship, *Madre de Dios*. Wallis to Curtiz, April 1:

> I just want to be sure that when you shoot the exterior of the boats again, the capture of the *Madre de Dios* by the slaves, that you do not have any battle or any battle scenes—but rather do this all in a sinister, mysterious fashion, with just shadowy figures coming over the rail, dropping down on the deck, crawling around corners of hatches, and stealing up on individuals and Spanish sailors. I'm sure this will be much more effective than if we again go into one of those battles with everybody wielding wooden swords around.
>
> Be sure that this is all done in sketchy lighting, as in the cabin scene where they burst in on the four Spanish soldiers around the table, they are all too brightly lighted, and those white, naked bodies, and those fat stomachs bouncing around, look anything but romantic, adventuresome men. Therefore, the less light you put on them, the better.

Meanwhile, Curtiz continued to embellish the opening battle scene between the two ships whenever he had an opportunity. His claim, from the preproduction days, that he would not be

13. James V. D'Arc, "Perfect Manners: An Interview with Olivia de Havilland," *American Classic Screen*, January/February, 1979, p. 9.

able to shoot a fight better than the one in *Captain Blood* was conveniently forgotten. Wallis unexpectedly kept seeing new shots when he screened the footage. On April 3 he wrote to Blanke and Wright:

> I notice in today's dailies that Mike is still shooting the battle scenes from the first battle, this time from other angles with the camera down in the foreground and the water in the tank and the guns still firing.
>
> I thought that we were all through with this battle. . . . I wonder how it is that Mike was permitted to schedule another day's work on the stage, making additional cuts of cannon firing, etc., when we had determined that we wouldn't make any more of this stuff. Will you gentlemen please enlighten me, as I would like to know just how long this is going to go on and what do I have to do to stop it.

(A year earlier, after several days of filming the big saloon brawl for *Dodge City* (1939), Wallis wrote Robert Lord and Tenny Wright: "I hope that Mike is through shooting the fight. . . . We have enough film already for two or three fights, and if he isn't through with everything by now, I want it stopped today.")

Wallis seems to have had a love-hate professional relationship with Curtiz. The communications to and about Curtiz from Wallis during the making of many of the director's films at Warners were similarly fault-finding and exasperated. Yet Wallis invariably chose Curtiz to handle many of the studio's better (and in many instances "bigger") projects. They were also quite friendly off the lot. It is apparent that the complementary relationship worked and usually yielded excellent results; Curtiz's embellishments of the big scenes in his pictures gave the productions a richness and visual excitement that contributed strongly to the timeless appeal they have. Wallis, on the other hand, was responsible for turning out an incredible number of films per year and had to equate time with money and operating efficiencies.

The last scheduled filming was the Panama episode, during which Thorpe and his men intercept a Spanish treasure train in the jungle and then later are intercepted themselves by other Spaniards. A few blocks from Warners' Burbank studio at the time was some studio property called 30 Acres. Anton Grot had the 500,000 square feet converted into a jungle (figure 18). Tropical plants, trees, and vines were brought to the area, and a four-and-a-half-inch water line was laid down, through which the land was flooded to create a swamp. To give the illusion of dense, dank heat, Grot provided fog machines that poured vapor over the "jungle" (cold water held the vapor close to the ground). The scenes at the Venta Cruz marketplace and the interior of the treasure-house were photographed on a set constructed for the 1939 *Juárez* at Warners' Calabasas Ranch several miles west of Burbank. The brief shots showing Thorpe and his party finally arriving at the shoreline from their escape through the swamps were filmed on the beach at Point Magu, northwest of Los Angeles. Other scenes depicting the exterior of a Dover street and dock, the palace garden (figure 14), palace gate (figure 23), and the exterior and interior of the chartmaker's shop were all shot on the backlot using standing sets.

While filming continued and the picture was being assembled and edited, the special effects department under Byron Haskin was preparing and filming the miniature ships (figure 2) for the distant shots that were eventually to be integrated into the sequences involving the closer angles of the full-scale ships already photographed on Stage 21. This unit also was responsible for the rear projection, or process (figure 17), and matte painting shots (figure 15). The ships, built at a scale of at least one inch to the foot, were carefully crafted to tie in with their full-scale counterparts.

Haskin told me that each miniature ship concealed a man, who from a prone position would guide the rudder and work the little inboard motors and the tiny cannons. Hans Koenekamp, regarded by Haskin as "the greatest trick man that ever lived," actually photographed the miniature ships on Warners' backlot lake (with painted sky background) and on the marine stage (with cyclorama background). The camera was rigged very close to the water level in a glass box and the ships were photographed in slow motion (approximately seventy frames per second) in order to create the proper illusion. For a realistic effect, it is important to have the miniatures as large in scale as possible—particularly when working in conjunction with water or fire, which are always potential giveaways in miniature work. The ships for *The Sea Hawk* were approximately eighteen feet long with sixteen-foot masts. Fortunately, by 1935 the effects department (then under Fred Jackman) had already experimented with a great many miniature ship shots for *Captain Blood*.

Finally, after sixty-seven days of shooting, unit manager Frank Mattison wrote:

Report for 4–19–40:
    Finished shooting at 9:40 P.M. last night. . . .
    Company is 19 days behind schedule.
    Finished Errol Flynn, Brenda Marshall and Jack LaRue in the cast.
    This finishes the picture with the exception of the inserts and pickup shots we are to do today, Saturday.

Postproduction

The highly regarded George Amy, Curtiz's favorite film editor, had been assigned from the beginning of shooting to cut the picture.

Erich Wolfgang Korngold, under contract to Warner Brothers, was set for the music—as it turned out, his last for a swashbuckler. Korngold previously had scored *Captain Blood, The Adventures of Robin Hood, The Private Lives of Elizabeth and Essex*, among other films, at Warners. His rich, romantic style, filled with melody, was particularly suited to the Flynn historical romances. He conceived his film scores as "operas without singing."

One charming melody that appeared to be sung on camera by Brenda Marshall, but which actually was dubbed by Sally Sweetland (nee Mueller), was developed by Korngold into an art song, a part of his Opus 38. To set the tropical scene and underline the apprehensive mood for the Panama sequence, the usual percussion complement of the Warners studio orchestra was augmented by tambourine, gourd, timbales, marimba, vibraphone, xylophone, tam-tam, temple blocks, glockenspiel, foot cymbal, and rumba drum. All this exotica, merged with shadowy saxophones, bunched pizzicato strings, and an occasional dash of Latin American syncopation, resulted in a musical episode unique for Korngold. A waltz he had written for *Danton*, an unproduced Warners film of 1936, was transformed into a quietly apprehensive march used for the jungle scenes. For the climactic duel-to-the-death between Thorpe and Wolfingham, Korngold composed a *tour de force* of rhythmic energy and exactitude that lasted one hundred seconds on the screen but took a total of three hours to record to the picture. And one of the most thrilling moments (musically and otherwise) follows the escape of Thorpe and his men from the galley. The music builds to a nervously excited climax and poises expectantly; then, as the crew members set sail for home on the captured Spanish ship, they break into a spirited chorus to voice their exultation at the newfound freedom. The *Sea Hawk* score is widely regarded as one of Korngold's best.

At one point, just before the original release of the film in the summer of 1940, serious thought was given to tinting the release prints of the Panama sequences green. Then Wallis wrote Jack Warner on July 11:

[Film editor] George Amy brings up a point that I think is very well taken. That is, that green is a cooling color, which it really is. . . . It is entirely possible that by putting this green tint on the film, we are apt to get just the opposite effect than we want, namely, a feeling of coolness instead of one of terrific heat.

An amber or perhaps a straw or yellowish tint might be even better, but I think in order to be safe we should let the print alone just as it is—black and white.

At least some of the initial release prints were sepia toned for the Panama sequences (green tinting, or toning, created problems in proper sound reproduction from the optical track).

In Release

On July 17 *The Sea Hawk* was previewed for the press and industry at Warners' Hollywood theater. It ran two hours and seven minutes. One month later the film was in first-run release with the length intact. Most reviewers praised the production in general and the action scenes specifically, but some thought the episodes of court intrigue tended to diminish the effect of the epic sweep. Philip T. Hartung in *Commonweal* (August 23, 1940) seemed to assess the picture most accurately:

Every now and then Hollywood crashes through with a good old blood-and-thunder adventure film that justifies whatever faith one may have in cinema's ability to excel when it stays within its proved medium. *The Sea Hawk* is such a picture. Warners' sagacious spending of the reputed million-and-a-half budget[14] shows up from every angle. . . . [It] will hold you spellbound for two hours and sweep your fancy back to the stirring days of "Good Queen Bess." . . . Some audiences may find the picture too long or the court scenes talky and detracting from the fast movement, but lovers of adventure and romance will eat up the whole thing from the first exciting sea battle to Elizabeth's final "Rise, Sir Geoffrey" [figure 25].

And, indeed, audiences did. Although *The Sea Hawk* lacked the perfect timing and fresh impact of the 1935 *Captain Blood* (this kind of subject having been dormant for years) and the legendary charm, color, and overall romantic perfection of *Robin Hood*, it was and is a first-rate example of its genre. And its appeal is perennial.

The formula is an entirely agreeable one. The hero is indeed a hero and the villains are most assuredly villains. If what we expect is what we get, it is all served expansively with the finest ingredients and in a relatively sophisticated manner. The audience is swept along and still seems willingly to enter into a suspension of disbelief. In the case of *The Sea Hawk*, familiarity does not breed contempt but rather pleasure.

Physically the production is much more opulent than the cautious, economy-minded *Captain Blood* of five years earlier. Although *Captain Blood* remains a charming and delightful film, it is archaic and quaint by comparison.

Flynn gave an excellent account of himself in *The Sea Hawk*— something he had not done in *Elizabeth and Essex*. Instead of the wide-open gallantry and less than assured style he displayed in *Captain Blood* or the impudently aggressive charmer he presented in *Robin Hood*, his Geoffrey Thorpe is cool and collected, gentlemanly, and shy and awkward in the presence of

14. The final negative cost was $1,701,211.

ladies—other than the queen, with whom he has a special relationship. At the time the film was initially released, there was some criticism (foreshadowed by Wallis's comments regarding some of the dailies) that his performance lacked fire and vigor and that the heroics were too understated. Flynn was deliberately trying to present a relatively restrained interpretation and had asked the producers and Koch to superimpose more dimension on the relatively stock heroic character. The performance wears well and is an interesting contrast to some of his previous roles. (We know that in fact Sir Francis Drake was by no means the swashbuckler. On the contrary, he had an instinctive courtesy and consideration and was exceptionally humane for the times in which he lived. But he was a strict disciplinarian and had outstanding qualities as a leader. He also had a boyish cheerfulness and a fearless nature. On the other side he could be hot-tempered, overbearing, and, when he thought it necessary, ruthless.)

To make sure that there was no confusion about the kind of film *The Sea Hawk* was, the studio prepared extensive advertising and exploitation that emphasized "Flynn in Action!" (These words were slashed across the cover of the pressbook.) In *Elizabeth and Essex* only a short time before, Flynn had not been in action. The choice of art and photographic elements in the ads obviously pointed up the *Captain Blood* derivatives, but to cover all bases the ads referred to "Errol Flynn in the thrill-swept story of the Robin Hood of the seas." ("An avenging bird of prey, he roamed the seven seas.") There were six-day serializations of the film's story available for possible use by newspapers, designer Orry-Kelly's sketches showing practical and modern adaptations of the film's costumes for *Vogue* and *Mademoiselle* magazines, a *Sea Hawk* model-builder kit, picture story book, paint book, a comic book depicting the story in action color pictures, and, of course, full-page ads in the fan magazines and some of the picture weeklies such as *Look* ("This is the matchless adventure that sets a new excitement-peak for the screen!").

Britain's reviews and audience response were at least as favorable as America's. The critics noted the parallels of the film with the dire European political events of 1939–40. Like the arrogant Hitler, King Philip of Spain (figure 1) in the script states that conquest will cease only when the entire world is under his control. The appeasement policy at Elizabeth's court was like the appeasement attempts in the late 1930s by Prime Minister Chamberlain and others. Elizabeth had her counselors who said that Spain would never attack, that the building of the Armada was not aimed at Britain, and that the safety of England depended upon yielding to all demands. During the writing, production, and release of *The Sea Hawk*, events in Europe moved rapidly. The shock of Hitler's conquest of Czechoslovakia (March 1939) and his callous violations of pledges made at Munich ended the appeasement policy of Britain. Plans were made to expand the fleet. By July of 1940 England was at bay, facing invasion. Only the British navy and a numerically weak air force barred the way across the English Channel.

The British release prints of *The Sea Hawk* contained a closing speech by Elizabeth not included in the edited American version. In part, the queen speaks of preparing the nation for war after trying to avert same. "But when the ruthless ambitions of a man threaten to engulf the world . . . we shall now make ready to meet the great Armada. . . . I pledge you . . . a navy foremost in the world—not only in our time, but in generations to come" (scenes 267–68).

The 1947 reissue of the film (with eighteen minutes out) did exceptionally well during the period following World War II when the box office was down and lots of revivals were making the rounds.

The Sea Hawk actually is an amalgamation of various elements from the preceding Warner-Flynn epics; a variation—albeit an exceptional one—on a theme (and a tested formula). Captain Blood is present, and so is Robin Hood, working amidst the physical assets of *Elizabeth and Essex*. And *The Sea Hawk*'s script and production are infinitely superior to those for most swashbucklers.

After the Hollywood preview of *The Sea Hawk*, Max Reinhardt, the world-renowned, innovative Austrian theatrical director, sent a congratulatory telegram to his friend and associate Henry Blanke. He concluded by saying, "It is a marvelous realization of our boyhood dreams."

Introduction

REFERENCES

Books

Andrews, Kenneth R. *Elizabethan Privateering*. London: Cambridge University Press, 1964.

Bell, Douglas. *Elizabethan Seamen*. Philadelphia: J. B. Lippincott, 1936.

Graham, Winston. *The Spanish Armadas*. Garden City, N.Y.: Doubleday, 1972.

Hume, Martin. *Two English Queens and Philip*. London: Methuen, 1908.

Jenkins, Elizabeth. *Elizabeth the Great*. New York: Coward-McCann, 1959.

Parker, Louis N. *Drake: A Pageant-Play*. New York: Dodd, Mead, 1925.

Richards, Jeffrey. *Swordsmen of the Screen: From Douglas Fairbanks to Michael York*. London: Routledge and Kegan Paul, 1977.

Williams, Neville. *All the Queen's Men: Elizabeth I and Her Courtiers*. New York: Macmillan, 1972.

Williamson, James A. *The Age of Drake*. London: Adam and Charles Black, 1946.

According to the Warner Brothers files, the books most used for research by Seton I. Miller and Howard Koch (and also consulted by the editor of this volume) were:

Anthony, Katharine. *Queen Elizabeth*. New York: Knopf, 1929.

Benson, E. F. *Sir Francis Drake*. New York: Harper, 1927.

Corbett, Julian. *Drake and the Tudor Navy*. New York: Longmans, Green, 1898.

Corbett, Julian. *Sir Francis Drake*. New York: Macmillan, 1890.

Davis, William Stearns. *Life in Elizabethan Days*. New York: Harper, 1930.

Froude, James Anthony. *English Seamen in the Sixteenth Century*. London: Longmans, 1928.

Gosse, Philip. *Hawkins: Scourge of Spain*. New York: Harper, 1930.

Gosse, Philip. *The History of Piracy*. London: Longmans, 1932.

Runciman, Sir Walter. *Drake, Nelson and Napoleon*. New York: Putnam, 1920.

Sabatini, Rafael. *Torquemada and the Spanish Inquisition*. New York: Houghton Mifflin, 1924.

Walling, R.A.J. *A Sea-Dog of Devon: A Life of Sir John Hawkins*. New York: J. Lane, 1907.

Wood, William. *Elizabethan Sea-Dogs: A Chronicle of Drake and His Companions*. New Haven: Yale University Press, 1918.

Unpublished Materials

Department of Special Collections, Doheny Library, University of Southern California: Early script versions of the 1940 *Sea Hawk* by Robert Neville (November 2, 1935) and Delmer Daves (April 17, 1936), and the 1924 *Sea Hawk* by J. G. Hawks (n.d.).

1. *King Philip II of Spain.*

2. *Newly photographed miniature ships were intercut with shots of full-scale ships in the sea battle.*

44

3. *Captain Geoffrey Thorpe.*

4. *Stock shot from* **Captain Blood** *(1935), used in the sea battle.*

45

5. *Stock shot from* The Divine Lady (1929), *used in the sea battle.*

6. *"I congratulate you, Captain. A very fortunate moment for the surrender."*

7. *Left to right: Don Alvarez, the Spanish ambassador; Carl Pitt, Thorpe's lieutenant; Doña Maria, and Captain Thorpe.*

8. *The development of a romance: Episode One (during the first third of the film).*

9. *The romance: Episode Two (about halfway through the film).*

10. *The romance: Episode Three (near the end of the film).*

11. *The royal procession at Queen Elizabeth's court.*

12. *Elizabeth I.*

13. *Captain Thorpe gifts the queen with his pet monkey.*

14. *The palace rose garden (backlot).*

15. *The* Albatross *at Dover. Bottom half of the frame was filmed on stage; top half is a matte painting.*

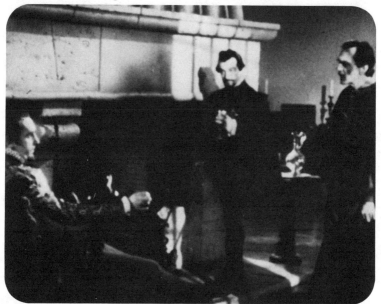

16. *Arch conspirators: Lord Wolfingham and Don Alvarez with their spy, Kroner.*

17. *The Isthmus of Panama. Miniature ship projected on large process screen.*
Fragmentary foreground set and actor on stage.

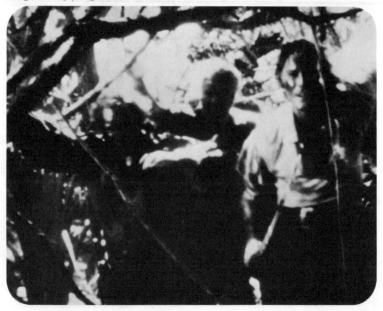

18. *Hacking their way out of the swamp (30 Acres—backlot).*

19. *The Inquisition Tribunal.*

20. *The palace council room.*

21. *Galley slaves.*

22. *The escape (on flooded stage with "ripple machine" effect on cyclorama sea background).*

23. *Echoes of* The Adventures of Robin Hood: *the Nottingham Gate and a pillar from Nottingham Castle transformed into the palace gate area (backlot).*

24. *Echoes of* The Adventures of Robin Hood: *the duel-to-the-death, complete with characteristic Curtiz shadows.*

25. *Echoes of* The Adventures of Robin Hood: *"I pronounce you a knight of the realm. Rise, Sir Geoffrey Thorpe!"*

The Sea Hawk

Screenplay

by

HOWARD KOCH

and

SETON I. MILLER

The Sea Hawk

Foreword

The story of this picture finds its origin in
the exploits of Sir Francis Drake, under
whose leadership Elizabethan England chal-
lenged the supremacy of the great empire of
Spain.[1]

FADE IN

1.   WALL OF THE SPANISH PALACE COUNCIL CHAMBER   DAY
Camera is focused on a part of the wall that is a map of
Spain in the year 1585. Camera begins to truck back,
revealing Spain as part of a huge map of the then known
world, drawn in the crude but decorative style of the
period. Spain and her far-flung possessions are indicated by a dark shade of gray, with the other countries
left in white. The map covers the entire wall of the richly
furnished council chamber. On a long, black oak council
table burn ornate candelabra. Gathered around it are six
richly dressed Spanish noblemen, among them Alvarez
and Peralta, and one strangely different—an ominous
black-hooded figure—one of the heads of the Inquisition.

At the head of the table, on a dais, sits the royal figure
of King Philip, a tall, haughty man with a lean, ascetic,
bearded face and intense, burning, black eyes.[2] He has
been speaking as the camera trucks back.

PHILIP:

. . . with our ships carrying our flag to the seven
seas, with our arms sweeping over Africa, the Near
East, and the Far West . . . invincible everywhere

59

but on our own doorstep. Northern Europe alone holds out against us. Why? Tell me why!

PERALTA:
Our depleted treasury, Your Majesty. An army can advance only to the end of its purse strings . . .

PHILIP:
Nonsense. The riches of the New World are limitless, and the New World is ours. That is not the reason, Peralta. Why do you not admit it? (He waits for the minister to speak, but Peralta is silent; low, tense voice.) The reason is a puny, rockbound island, as barren and as treacherous as her queen, who secretly gives aid to our enemies, while her pirates plunder our commerce. You know as well as I that we will never keep northern Europe in submission until we have a reckoning with England.

PERALTA:
But it is not yet time, Your Majesty. Not until the Armada is built.

2.   CLOSE SHOT   PHILIP

PHILIP (rising; speaks impatiently):
Time! The destiny of Spain cannot wait upon the fitness of time. I have but one life. And that life is all too short for me to fulfill that destiny. (Turns to a nobleman at his right.) Don Alvarez . . .

ALVAREZ:
Sire?

PHILIP:
You will proceed at once to England as my ambassador. There you will assure— (ironically) the queen of my patience and continued affection . . . to allay any suspicions regarding our plans.

ALVAREZ:
As you wish, Your Majesty.

PHILIP:
>   With England conquered, nothing can stand in our way.

He faces the wall map, moves slowly toward it. His voice becomes mystical. The camera pans to the map. While Philip speaks, his shadow creeps up on the map, blends with the dark gray of Spain, and spreads over the areas as he calls them by name.

PHILIP (over scene):
>   Northern Africa, Europe as far east as the Urals, the New World to the north and to the south, and west to the Pacific, and over the Pacific to China and the Indies, will our empire spread . . . One day before my death we shall sit here and gaze upon this wall. It will have ceased to be a map of the world. It will be Spain.

By now the shadow of Philip darkens the entire world.

DISSOLVE TO:

3.   SHIP STANDARD STAFF FLAG   DAY
In the late afternoon sun a flag flutters feebly from the staff—the embroidered gold banner of Spain. Camera pans down over the mizzen, to the quarterdeck of a large Spanish galleass.[3] The camera trucks toward two richly dressed Spaniards who are talking at the rail. One is Don Alvarez, last seen in the council of Philip. The other is Captain López, commanding the ship. They are glancing up at the sails, in which there is barely enough wind for "steerage way."

LÓPEZ:
>   I regret our slow passage, Your Excellency, but it seems our sail cannot entice the wind.

ALVAREZ:
>   Then we shall not reach England by Wednesday?

LÓPEZ (shrugs):
>   Perhaps—if the galley holds out.

ALVAREZ:

Captain López, it is extremely important that my niece be presented to the queen before her new maids of honor are chosen.

LÓPEZ:

They say that Elizabeth surrounds herself with beauty in the hope that it may be contagious.

They both smile, and the camera pans with them to the opposite side of the quarterdeck, where Doña Maria, niece of Alvarez, is playing battledore and shuttlecock with her English companion, Miss Latham.

LÓPEZ (over scene):

Your niece will have no trouble meeting the queen's requirements.

As López speaks the last line the camera trucks toward Maria and Miss Latham. Maria is a beautiful, spirited girl; Miss Latham a very proper English lady, rather stiff, but with a quick sense of humor. Maria makes a beautiful retrieve and sends the bird out of her companion's reach.

MISS LATHAM (puffing from her effort):

Maria, you might put it once where I can reach it.

MARIA (innocently):

You said you needed exercise, Martha.

MISS LATHAM:

Well, I've had it. Enough for the whole trip.

MARIA:

Oh, just one more game, please . . . while the wind's down. (Laughs.) You said the English never leave the field defeated.

MISS LATHAM:

Well, occasionally they stop for breath.

She serves the bird. Maria returns it. It goes high in the air. We follow it aloft, then leave it to focus on a Spanish sailor who is climbing to the "top" on the mizzenmast.

CUT TO:

4.   TWO SHOT   ALVAREZ AND LÓPEZ
at rail of quarterdeck. Alvarez is speaking.

ALVAREZ:

But why those extra precautions, Captain? Isn't the forecastle lookout enough?

LÓPEZ:

I'm responsible for your safety, Your Excellency, and we're entering the lanes of the English pirates.

ALVAREZ:

How interesting! If your men spy any of the ships, I wish you'd let me know.

LÓPEZ:

Like hawks, Don Alvarez, they're on you before you see them. They say the devil blows in their sails.

ALVAREZ (laughs):

Surely you don't believe those myths, Captain . . . At any rate, they would hardly dare molest a ship with His Majesty's ambassador aboard. It would be as much as their heads are worth when the news reached the queen.

LÓPEZ (smiles enigmatically):

Perhaps . . . Excuse me, Your Excellency, but the breeze is still slackening. (He walks to the forward rail and calls to the main deck.) Bos'n! Order the beat raised eight counts. (Camera pans down to the bos'n on the main deck.)

BOS'N:

At once, Captain. (He calls through the grating of the hatch, down to the hold.) There below! Raise the beat of the oars! Eight counts!

Camera pans down the hold following the voice. Framed in the hatch are the head and shoulders of the Spanish slave master.

SLAVE MASTER:
> Eight counts, señor.

CUT TO:

5. THE GALLEY ROOM   FULL SHOT
Along the hull on each side of a fairly wide center floor is a sunken pit, containing rowers' benches. Through openings in the hull on each side come the long, heavy handles of twenty oars (forty to the ship). There are three men to each oar, and each pull of the oar is a horrible effort. The men are all chained to the benches. They are naked, except for loincloths, bearded, unkempt, scarred, their faces drawn and haggard, but they are not criminal types. On the contrary, they are nearly all fine types, mostly Englishmen, the majority of them English middle class, with good strong faces, many of them seamen. Here and there a patrician, intellectual type, all of them ground down to the tortured status of animals.

As we come to the scene they are rowing a slow stroke. The rhythm is being beaten out on a heavy wooden block at one end by a gross-faced Spanish sailor using a large wooden gavel. Two hard-faced Spaniards are moving slowly up and down with long whips. The slave master hurries down the steps in foreground, barking.

SLAVE MASTER:
> Raise the beat. Eight counts! (The whippers and the timekeeper come alive, the timekeeper beginning to beat faster. The whippers pace the runway, fingering the whips, watching to see that the slaves obey.) Faster! Bend to it!

Camera moves in closer to the galley slaves. In their exhausted condition, it is punishing cruelty to pull the heavy oars faster, but the men manage to raise their stroke to the higher beat. Camera pans over the group, staying on a white-haired old seaman with faded blue eyes, William Tuttle. Next to him is a husky, fine-looking man, Martin Barrett. The older man seems in an exhausted trance as he pulls on the oar. Suddenly his face lights up.

TUTTLE (whispers to Barrett):
I know where we are . . .

BARRETT (whispers back as he pulls):
You can't tell, William. We haven't known for months.

TUTTLE:
I am sure this time. Feel the motion . . . the cross swell. Only one place like that . . . (His face glowing.) The English Channel . . .

BARRETT (repeats wonderingly):
The English Channel . . .

The man on his right hears it and passes it on as an accepted fact. The words "English Channel" stir through the rows of exhausted slaves.

Suddenly there is a crash on the deck above, followed by shots, the blowing of a trumpet, the clanking of arms, and rushing feet on the deck. The galley slaves look up at the ceiling, slowly realize the import of the noise.

TUTTLE:
An attack!

BARRETT (in a loud whisper):
Hold back on your oars . . . pretend to row.

A whip curves around his back like a snake. The camera pulls back to show the Spaniards—tense and expectant. Suddenly the bos'n's voice comes down the hatch from above.

BOS'N'S VOICE (over scene):
> Raise the beat! Quick, do you hear? Raise it to twenty. Drive them.

The slave master and his two mates are galvanized into action. They move up and down the runway, lashing the men savagely.

WHIPPERS (ad lib, interspersed with lashes):
> Pull, you! Get together! *Together* I said! Put some weight on that oar! Do you hear that count? Faster! Faster, you British dogs!

Despite the cruel beating, the slaves only put on a show of rowing hard. Their sweeps are ineffectual and out of unison as they do their best to impede the ship's progress. Over the shouts of the whippers, the cracks of the whips, and the beats of the timekeeper, there continues from above an increasing din.

6.   FULL SHOT   MAIN DECK OF THE GALLEASS
from the angle of the quarterdeck. The main deck is in a frenzy of preparation. Camera pans over cannon being moved into place, crew bringing up ammunition, soldiers putting on armor.

LÓPEZ'S VOICE (off scene):
> Lower away boarding nets! Master gunner, load your port sakers with chain shot . . . ! Elevate the pieces and lay at his rigging . . . Quartermaster, four points to starboard . . .

Camera comes to rest on Captain López and Alvarez on the forward rail of the quarterdeck. López is shouting down orders to the officers below. There is continued tumult off scene.

LÓPEZ (turns to a military officer nearby):
> Man the castles with your musketeers and tell them to look to their matches! (He turns to Alvarez, who is gazing off scene.) I must ask you to remain with

the ladies in the cabin, Don Alvarez. It will not be safe on deck.

ALVAREZ:
The pirates won't dare attack when they see the king's emblem.

LÓPEZ:
Guns may stop them; nothing else.

A second officer runs up to them and salutes.

OFFICER:
Señor Captain, it is Thorpe's ship!

LÓPEZ (visibly startled):
Thorpe? No . . . no, it is impossible. Only a month ago he was at San Domingo.

OFFICER:
The breath of satan . . . (Crosses himself quickly.) They all turn toward the outer rail, gazing off scene.) Look, Señor Captain, on the staff . . . The banner of the *Albatross!*

VOICES (over scene, at first loud, then receding as the dreaded word travels down the main deck):
The *Albatross* . . . The *Albatross* . . . *Albatross* . . . *Albatross* . . .[4]

7.   FULL SHOT   THE ALBATROSS   (IN MINIATURE)
In the distance, sharply outlined against a sunset sky, is an English sailing ship, no oars, its square-rigged sails well filled.

                                                    CUT TO:

8.   MED. SHOT   OF THE BANNER
that flies at the mainmast peak, a flag with a spread-winged albatross. The camera pans over the rigging where a monkey is swinging in the ropes, indifferent to what goes on below him, then continues to pan down to the main deck of the ship, where the crew are crouched

The Sea Hawk

along the starboard cannons, their excited attention riveted on what we know to be the galleass off scene. Most of the men are stripped to the waist. The camera pans slowly along the starboard rail, holding just long enough for terse bits of conversation down the line. The men continue to gaze off scene as they speak.

MARTIN BURKE:
The Spaniard mounts forty guns if she mounts one! (Taps the gun nearest him.) Maybe she's too big a bite for the size of our teeth.

ELI MATSON:
Did you ever see a Spaniard the cap'n couldn't swallow whole?

MONTY PRESTON:
The cap'n's got the Spaniards bewitched, that's wot 'e 'as.

The camera now moves up along the quarterdeck rail where Oliver Scott, the first mate, and Carl Pitt, lieutenant, stand ready to go into action. Beside Pitt stands Arnold Cross, gunner of the starboard quarterdeck cannon.

OLIVER SCOTT (grins as he gazes):
The *Albatross* isn't a bird you can run away from. We're suckin' the wind out of the Spaniard's sails.

CARL PITT (grins back; gestures toward the cannon):
If it's air they're lookin' for, the old lady can put a draft through their stern quick enough. (He calls off and above him.) How about it, Cap'n? Shall we let them have a round?

THORPE'S VOICE (sharply, from off scene):
You will fire when I tell you to.

CARL (meekly):
Yes, sir.

Scott smiles at Carl's chagrined look. Obviously no liberties can be taken when Thorpe's tone becomes crisp and formal.

Camera pans up to Captain Francis Thorpe,[5] who stands on the poop deck glancing off scene. In contrast to the ordinary conception of a pirate, Thorpe gives the impression of a young but extremely able sea commander. His official exterior is a trifle stern, but an engaging human quality frequently dispels his protective shell of aloofness. His speech is clipped, sometimes edged with a biting irony. His manner is offhand and casual, never heroic even on heroic occasions.

THORPE:
> Hail the Spaniards, Mr. Scott . . . *Suggest* that they strike their colors.

The camera pulls to a wider angle that includes the three officers.

SCOTT:
> Yes, sir. (He calls off scene through a speaking trumpet of the period.) Señor Captain! Lower your flag . . . ! Lower your flag!

CARL (low voice, to Scott):
> It would be just like 'em to surrender and spoil all the fun . . .

SCOTT (calls even louder):
> Do you hear me? Strike your flag!

9.   FULL SHOT   THE GALLEASS   (IN MINIATURE)
from angle of the *Albatross*. The Spanish boat suddenly answers the demand to surrender with a broadside. We see white puffs of smoke from her hull.

10.   MED. SHOT   QUARTERDECK OF THE ALBATROSS
One lone cannonball from the Spanish broadside shatters some rigging above their heads. Carl roars with laughter.

CARL:

> One lone cannonball out of a whole broadside.
> Oh—

He stops suddenly as he feels Thorpe's gaze upon him. This brings a slight smile to the captain's lips, hidden from his officers.

THORPE:

> Their marksmanship's as bad as their manners. Show them how to dip their colors, Mr. Pitt.

CARL (adjusting the sights of the cannon):

> Aye, Cap'n! . . . Ready, Cross; let the old lady give 'em a lesson!

CROSS:

> Aye, Lieutenant.

Cross lights the torch and applies it to the powder. The cannon roars.

CUT TO:

11. FULL SHOT OF THE GALLEASS (MINIATURE)
from Thorpe's angle. Cannonball snaps off the main-mast near its peak. The golden banner of Spain drops to the water and a lusty cheer goes up off scene from the crew of the *Albatross*.

12. SPANISH SHIP MED. SHOT (STOCK)[6]
from the poop deck. We see gear and rigging of the mainmast crash down on soldiers and crew in the waist of the ship. A cannon from the quarterdeck answers the shot from the *Albatross*.

CUT TO:

13. FULL SHOT TWO SHIPS (IN MINIATURE) (STOCK CAPTAIN BLOOD)[7]
The two ships engage each other in a running fight with the *Albatross* slowly, slowly closing in. Alternately the ships belch fire and smoke amid a bedlam of noise.

DISSOLVE TO:

14. MED. SHOT   THE ALBATROSS QUARTERDECK   DAY

Thorpe stands on the forward rail, looking down into the main deck. Beside him are Carl and a smoking gun. A seaman, Burke, rushes up to Thorpe.

BURKE:
> The Spaniard's listing, Cap'n. We must've hit her below the waterline.

THORPE:
> All right, Burke. (He leans over the rail and speaks to the men below. His voice is low and tense.) Cease firing, men. It's cutlasses now. We're going to board her.

A cheer goes up below. There is a bustle of preparation—men getting their cutlasses and knives. We get the effect of a completely loyal crew, excited and happy at the prospect of a hand-to-hand fight.

15. CLOSE SHOT   ELI

The small Cockney is sharpening an oversized cutlass. He grins to Burke who stands near him.

ELI:
> A sharp edge for cuttin' the gold buttons off 'is lordship, the Spanish captain's doublet.

16. MED. SHOT   QUARTERDECK RAIL AND WAIST OF ALBATROSS

The men laugh. Thorpe pretends not to hear.

THORPE:
> Boarding irons ready? (Several "ayes" from the crew. He turns back to the men.) No one is to board the Spaniard until I give the order. Is that clear?

AD LIB SHOUTS (from the men on the main deck):
> Aye, Captain! Aye, sir! Aye, sir!

THORPE:
> Starboard, Mr. Scott . . . into them hard!

71

He opens a door under the quarterdeck, calls in to the navigator.

SCOTT:
Two points to starboard!

VOICE (from below):
Two points to starboard.

CUT TO:

17.   FULL SHOT   THE TWO SHIPS   (MINIATURE)   DAY
The two ships are nearly together. The *Albatross* is closing in on the galleass. The firing has ceased. The Spanish oars are still moving feebly as the boat sags visibly on her port side. The *Albatross* reaches the Spanish oars.

CUT TO:

18.   SIDE OF GALLEASS AND OARS   DOWN SHOT   (MINIATURE)
as the hull of the *Albatross* sweeps against the oars, stopping them, shoving some down, breaking others off.

19.   MED. SHOT   ALBATROSS MAIN DECK
as the two ships come close together. Most of the *Albatross* crew are at the starboard rail, tensely waiting for Thorpe's command to board the other ship. However, Eli is too eager for the fray. Cutlass in hand, he leaps over both rails and lands single-handed on the galleass deck.

THORPE (quickly, as he takes in Eli's foolhardy act):
Ready, men! Over the rail!

Thorpe jumps across, Carl, Scott, and the others close behind him.

20.   WAIST OF SPANISH SHIP   FULL SHOT   (STOCK CAPTAIN BLOOD)
as grappling hooks bite into the Spanish rail and the English pour over the rail with a roar, above which is heard the shout.

VOICE:
For the queen and England!

21.   MAIN DECK   QUICK FLASHES
of Thorpe and Carl wading through the Spaniards to
reinforce the sorely pressed Eli, who, with his back to
the rail, is wielding his cutlass like a dervish dancer.
Thorpe and Carl reach him in time, and the Spaniards
are pressed back;
of Scott battling two of them with his cutlass but suddenly and surprisingly, while using the cutlass on one,
he swings a short, terrific left-hand punch at the other
man who is closer, and the latter goes down like a log.

22.   GROUP   AT THORPE   MED. CLOSE TRUCKING SHOT
As Thorpe battles he sees the Spanish captain and battles through to him, engaging him, backing him with
brilliant swordplay. We truck with them as they battle
clear of the surging crowd. Thorpe, pressing the attack,
forces López up the stairs to the quarterdeck.

THORPE (as they duel):
Your ship is sinking, Captain.

LÓPEZ (grimly):
Then we shall go down together.

THORPE:
Heroic, but impractical . . . We English are a practical people . . . I have no intention of going down
with you. (Out of the corner of his eye, he catches
sight of Carl on the main deck, just below the quarterdeck rail. He lets López work him over close to
the rail so that he can call down to Carl while holding the captain at bay.) Quick . . . the trumpeter
. . . near the forecastle . . .

CARL (looks up at the captain):
Aye, Cap'n.

He starts off toward the forecastle. Thorpe now savagely renews the attack on the Spanish captain, who attempts to parry but is gradually pressed back against an outside rail of the quarterdeck. Camera pans down to the waist of the ship and through various portions of the battling men. The crew of the *Albatross* are pushing the Spaniards into the midst of the fallen rigging, shot down by cannon fire. We see Eli reach down, jerk a section of the rigging, and upset three Spaniards who have closed in on an English sailor. Camera pans to the forecastle where Carl is in pursuit of the Spanish trumpeter. The Spaniard attempts to escape into the forecastle, but Carl's knife, thrown from a distance of ten feet, buries itself in the forecastle door, just grazing the man's neck. The trumpeter stops in terror and Carl is on him with a cutlass on his throat.

CARL:

> Sound the surrender! (The trumpeter hesitates; the sword point presses harder.) Hurry . . . while there's still breath in your belly!

Carl draws his sword back as the Spaniard reaches for his trumpet.

23.   TWO SHOT   THORPE AND LÓPEZ

Just as Thorpe has the captain pressed back against the rail, helpless, the trumpet sounds clearly over the fighting. Thorpe draws back his sword.

THORPE:

> A very fortunate moment for the surrender, Captain. I congratulate you.[8]

The camera pans over the ship, where the fighting comes to a sudden end. The English break out in a cheer as Thorpe appears above them at the quarterdeck rail. Thorpe quickly vaults over the rail to the floor of the main deck where he directs proceedings with rapid commands.

THORPE:
> Stack their weapons and herd them forward! Mr. Scott, you'll take charge!

SCOTT (steps forward):
> Aye, sir.

THORPE:
> You, Rollins, take some men and get the slaves out! Get hammers and hurry!

A half-dozen men start for the hatch. At this moment Thorpe sees Eli Matson, who is obviously endeavoring to keep out of sight.

THORPE (very quietly):
> Come here, Matson.

ELI (approaching the captain with considerable reluctance):
> Aye, Captain?

THORPE:
> That was very brave of you . . . trying to take this ship single-handed. (A relieved grin begins to spread over Eli's face, but it quickly vanishes as Thorpe's voice suddenly changes to steel.) Brave but foolhardy! Disobey my orders, will you? . . . Preston—

PRESTON (steps forward):
> Yes, sir?

THORPE:
> Take this man to our brig and see that he's put in chains. (He turns on his heel, leaving the chastened Eli to be led away by his fellow sailor.)

24.   MED. SHOT   THORPE AND PART OF CREW
who are rather subdued after the incident of Eli's arrest.

THORPE (notices their crestfallen looks):
> Very well done, all the rest of you! (The men look

happier as Thorpe's stern mood lifts.) Mr. Pitt, you come with me—and Burke and Logan.

CARL:
Aye, sir.

THORPE (his hand on Carl's shoulder as they turn toward the quarterdeck):
Thank you for . . . convincing the trumpeter.

Carl and the two sailors grin as they follow Thorpe through the door to the stern quarters.

25.   OMITTED

26.   FULL SHOT   THE GALLEY
where the Englishmen are running down the stairs with hammers in their hands. The slaves are slumped down, fearful, uncertain. Thorpe's men start swiftly striking off the chains, and a slow realization that they are being set free begins to dawn in the numbed minds of the slaves.
                                                    CUT TO:

27.   THE SMALL VESTIBULE IN THE STERN QUARTERS
outside the passengers' cabins, which Thorpe, Carl, and the others are searching with swift, routine efficiency. They come out of one door and go to the next one, except for one man who starts toward the deck with a small chest. The next door appears to be locked, and the other two men exchange a look of minor irritation as they set themselves to the routine of smashing it in. A steady stream of the English sailors can be seen passing from the storeroom to the deck with chests, sacks, barrels, etc., and back for more.

THORPE (calls to one of them):
Hey, Boggs! What's the cargo?

BOGGS:
Cloth mostly, Cap'n . . . a little gold.

THORPE:
You'll have to be quick . . . She's settling fast.

CUT TO:

28.   INSIDE THE CABIN
Maria's cabin, which is small but luxuriously furnished. Facing the door stand Alvarez, Maria, and Miss Latham. The door is fast giving way. Alvarez waits with evident indecision, Maria proudly defiant, Miss Latham anxious and apologetic. The door falls in with a splintering crash. The Englishmen enter and start to go to work as though there had been no interruption. Thorpe only takes casual notice of the occupants of the room as he motions them to one side.

THORPE:
Stand over there, please . . . Burke, you go through the drawers.

ALVAREZ (clenching the hilt of his sword):
Are you the captain of these pirates?

THORPE (giving Alvarez no attention, he addresses an order to Danny Logan, who has followed them in):
Logan, give Mr. Pitt a hand with that chest.

DANNY:
Yes, sir. (He helps Carl drag out a heavy chest.)

THORPE:
Pile the . . . contraband over here, Burke.

ALVAREZ (in a helpless fury):
I am King Philip's ambassador, Don Alvarez de Córdoba de Sev—

THORPE (turns to Alvarez briefly):
Pardon me, sir, we're pressed for time. Your ship's sinking.

At the mention of the word "sinking" Maria and Miss Latham cling closer together. The fury of Alvarez is impotent against the casual, businesslike attitude of the Englishmen. Carl has pried open the chest, finds a case of jewels on the top.

CARL:
Look, Cap'n—not bad.

MARIA (gives an involuntary gasp):
Uncle, my jewels.

Her uncle's hand on her arm restrains her from any protests, but Miss Latham cannot stand it any longer. She faces Carl with blazing indignation.

MISS LATHAM:
Don't you dare touch those jewels!

As Carl glances up into the stern countenance of Miss Latham, his face suddenly breaks out into an incongruous smile of recognition.

CARL:
An Englishwoman! By heavens, an Englishwoman!

MISS LATHAM (snaps out at him):
But not very proud of it at the moment.

CARL (still beams; paying no attention to her anger, tossing the jewel box into the pile of plunder):
I haven't laid eyes on an Englishwoman since . . .

THORPE (sharply):
Mr. Pitt, you'll have time to discuss that later. (To Burke.) Burke, you can take the first load up on deck.

BURKE:
Aye, sir. (Starts to pick up some of the spoils.)

MISS LATHAM (more concerned with the proprieties than the actual danger facing her and her friends):
Your Excellency . . . Maria, these aren't typical Englishmen; please don't think—

DANNY (a sawed-off, battle-scarred seaman who is hoisting a box of Maria's possessions on his shoulder):
> That's right, they oin't all so 'andsome as us, by gawd.

He winks at Miss Latham but, catching Thorpe's eye, he quickly fades out of the cabin behind Burke. Thorpe turns to Alvarez as the search is completed.

THORPE:
> You and the ladies better get your things together and board my ship. This one isn't going to float much longer . . .

Maria looks around the room in dismay at her "things," which are strewn all over it.

CARL:
> We sure ran into luck, Captain.

He looks up with a significant glance from the plunder to Miss Latham.

ALVAREZ:
> Captain Thorpe—I demand to know exactly what your intentions are.

THORPE (turns back to Alvarez):
> My intentions? To land you safely at your English port, señor.

MARIA (takes a step toward Thorpe, her eyes flashing):
> I'll not go on your ship! I'd rather drown . . .

Thorpe looks at her appraisingly for just a moment, but turns to speak to Carl, who is carrying the jewel casket toward the door.

THORPE:
> Mr. Pitt, if the young lady doesn't change her mind, change it for her. See that she's carried aboard.

Maria and her uncle are too furious to speak. Thorpe and Carl turn toward the door.

CUT TO:

29. FULL SHOT THE MAIN DECK
where the list of the sinking ship is now very decided. The Spanish officers and crew (Captain López among them) are being guarded by Scott and some of the English crew. A steady stream of treasure chests, bolts of cloth, sacks, barrels, and arms is being loaded across the rails onto the *Albatross*. The camera pans over to Thorpe, who is now supervising the loading. Camera trucks close to Thorpe.

THORPE:
Quickly there . . . ! Clear the decks . . . This way . . .

At this moment Alvarez, Miss Latham, and Maria, followed by Carl, who watches her closely, appear on the main deck. They are stopped in their progress by the released galley slaves, who come stumbling out on deck, ragged and bleeding. Some of them are still too dazed to realize their freedom. They still drag their feet that are no longer chained. They take deep lungsful of the clean air; they look around at the deck as though they were in a totally unfamiliar world.

THORPE:
We'll get these men off first . . . Mr. Pitt, Burke, the rest of you—help them over the rail . . . see that they don't fall.

William Tuttle sees Thorpe giving orders, recognizes him, and makes for him.

THORPE (looks at the bedraggled figure, finally recognizes him):
Why, Tuttle . . . ! It must be four years since we sailed together . . .

TUTTLE:
>It's four years since I've been on an English ship, sir.

THORPE (very kindly):
>Soon you'll be in England. (Includes the rest of the slaves.) Now on board with you, and I'll see you catch up on your grog rations.

SLAVES (ad lib):
>Thank you, sir . . . thank you . . . thank you . . .

Camera pans to Maria, her uncle, and Miss Latham, who stand on the main deck aft, with a leather casket of possessions. They have been watching the byplay between Tuttle and Thorpe and are now watching the galley slaves being led across the tilting deck.

30.   CLOSE SHOT   MARIA   ON DECK
Maria's eyes are wide with shock. It is evident that she has never seen or imagined a sight like the one presented by the bewildered slaves. Camera pulls back to include Thorpe, noticing her reaction. When she becomes aware of his glance, her attitude changes immediately to haughty composure. Thorpe turns to Alvarez, who stands beside Maria and Miss Latham.

THORPE:
>As soon as the slaves are transferred you may take the ladies to the *Albatross*.

ALVAREZ:
>This is an insult to His Majesty! I board your ship under protest, Captain Thorpe!

THORPE (with a gesture toward the slaves):
>At least, señor, you will find English hospitality better than they found Spanish.

31.   RAIL OF MAIN DECK
where the last of the slaves are being helped over to the

Albatross followed by Don Alvarez, Maria, and Miss Latham.

THORPE (calls out):
Abandon ship! Over the railing, everybody!

Like monkeys the Spanish clamber over the rail all along the main deck, and jump to the waist of the *Albatross*. Following them come Scott and his men, who were guarding them. Thorpe waits for Captain López to go over the rail, but the Spaniard hesitates, turns to his captor.

LÓPEZ:
I am still the captain, sir . . . ?

THORPE (understandingly):
Of course . . .

He vaults easily over the rail to the *Albatross*. López stands on the slanting deck of his sinking ship, and his eyes sweep her proud structure for the last time. Then he mounts the rail and over to the other boat.

32.   THE TWO SHIPS   (IN MINIATURE)
as the boarding irons are released and the boats drift apart. The galleass settles fast. From the distance we see the shadowy hull raise in the air and sink beneath the water.

33.   FULL SHOT   WAIST OF ALBATROSS
The English crew, gathered on the starboard side of the ship, set up a cheer as they see the Spanish boat go down (off scene). The camera pans to the stern section of the main deck where Alvarez, Maria, Miss Latham, the Spanish officers and crew are watching the spectacle in grim silence. Camera pans up to the starboard side of the quarterdeck as Thorpe hastily descends the stairs from the poop deck to the quarterdeck rail.

THORPE (calls out sharply below him):
Enough of that!

The cheering of the English sailors stops abruptly. The eyes of both ships' companies turn up toward the captain.

34. FULL SHOT   MAIN AND QUARTERDECKS   STARBOARD SIDE

THORPE (in a milder tone):
For the rest of the trip both crews will lay aside past differences. Spanish sailors will have freedom of the forecastle. (Wryly.) Except for the armory and powder magazine. (There is a laugh from his own men and a few smiles on the part of the Spaniards as the tension is relaxed. Thorpe continues in a gentler voice.) Those of you lately called "slaves" will have no duties aboard this ship.

Camera pans to the ragged group of freed galley slaves, still bewildered and huddled together on the port side of the main deck. Their drawn faces look gratefully up to Thorpe as he speaks to them.

THORPE'S VOICE (over scene):
If any of you are still for the sea, we have berths on our ships for willing men. By now you know the purpose of the Sea Hawks⁹ . . . in our own way to serve England and the queen.

A great cheer goes up from the entire English company as the camera pans back to Thorpe, who walks to the quarterdeck stairs directly above Don Alvarez, the Spanish guests, and officers.

THORPE:
Your Excellency, if you and your party will come this way, we'll make you as comfortable as our overcrowded quarters permit.

Alvarez bows curtly, starts up the stairs, followed by

Maria, Miss Latham, López, and two other Spanish officers. Behind them comes Oliver Scott.

THORPE (to Alvarez):
Mr. Scott will take you to your rooms.

Alvarez again bows in silent acknowledgment.

LÓPEZ:
And we shall be free when we get to the shore, Captain?

THORPE:
Naturally. We have no Inquisition in England. [10]

ALVAREZ (grimly):
No, we understand you believe in direct action.

THORPE (smiles slightly):
I find it more effective than . . . shall we say, diplomacy . . . Don Alvarez, I know how you feel. But fate has brought us together. Let us make the best of it.

DISSOLVE TO:

35.   INSERT
A large barrel marked Madeira, Vintage 1572. The camera pulls back to show the barrel lifted on the shoulders of a sailor stripped to the waist, who is carrying it out of the hatchway onto the main deck. Behind him comes a line of sailors carrying more wine barrels and huge silver platters with steaming fish and game.

36–37. OMITTED

38.   MED. LONG SHOT   A SMALLER TABLE ON THE
      QUARTERDECK
where Thorpe is the host to the officers of the *Albatross*, the Spanish officers, Alvarez, Maria, and Miss Latham. [11]

39. MED. CLOSE SHOT   THORPE AND GROUP
at head of table.

THORPE:

. . . The secret of victory, Captain López, is to make your enemy anticipate defeat. (Turns to Alvarez.) Your Excellency, more wine?

ALVAREZ (briefly):
No, thank you.

LÓPEZ (unbending):
I must compliment you on the wine, Captain Thorpe. Nowhere have I tasted better.

THORPE (smiles):
There is no better wine than Madeira. (López raises his eyebrows.) Where did we . . . pick this up, Mr. Pitt?

Camera pans down the table, centering on Carl, Miss Latham, and Scott.

CARL (grins):
From a galleon off Vera Cruz, Cap'n.

SCOTT:
No, it wasn't, Carl. This was out of the governor's cellar at Cartagena.

CARL:
No, Cartagena was all those Portuguese cheeses, remember?

MISS LATHAM (thawing a little in the company of Englishmen):
But there's no cheese like Cheddar, is there, Mr. Pitt?

CARL:
No place like England for anything, to my way of thinking. You must've been pretty lonesome in a

heathen country like Spain. (Realizing Maria is on his left.) Beg your pardon, miss . . .

Maria gives Carl not the slightest sign that she has heard.

MISS LATHAM:
Spain is an old country with a very rich culture. (Carl and Scott exchange puzzled looks as Miss Latham continues.) In fact, there is much in Spain we English can profit by.

CARL (giving Scott a sly wink):
We're doing our best, ma'am.

40.   MED. SHOT   THE ENTIRE TABLE
favoring Thorpe and group at head.

LÓPEZ (fingering a silver spoon):
I've also been admiring your table silver, Captain.

ALVAREZ:
No doubt another of the captain's . . . acquisitions.

THORPE (frankly):
Yes, if you look at the back, you will perhaps recognize the coat of arms of the Spanish viceroy of San Domingo.

This is too much for Maria. She rises angrily from the table. Thorpe immediately springs to his feet to anticipate her action. The others at the table, not knowing quite what to do, follow suit.

ALVAREZ (sternly):
Maria!

She holds for a moment.

THORPE (quickly):
I propose that we drink to the health of . . .

MARIA (turns on him with blazing scorn):
> I don't drink with thieves and pirates! (She turns
> and starts off. Thorpe's voice stops her.)

THORPE (to cover the general embarrassment; lifts his
goblet as if nothing had happened):
> The health I was about to propose is to Her Majesty,
> the Queen of England.

The English at the table drink heartily. The Spanish with
less enthusiasm. Maria is forced to resume her seat as
she drinks the toast. On the byplay between them we
hear

VOICES:
> To the queen! The queen! The queen!

DISSOLVE TO:

41. COAT OF ARMS
over the doorway of the queen's council chamber in the
palace.

42. CLOSE SHOT   ELIZABETH
sitting imperiously on her small throne chair in the
council chamber. She is in one of her temperamental
tirades.

ELIZABETH:
> Build a fleet! Build a fleet! Always the same advice.
> (Ironically.) Perhaps my lord admiral will also ad-
> vise where to get the money to pay for it.

As she speaks the camera pans back to reveal Burleson,
a gentle, white-haired man who is lord of the admiralty.
Pacing up and down in back of the queen is her lord
chancellor, Wolfingham, a clever, sinister, towering
man whose designs are concealed under an apparent
deference to Elizabeth's notionate opinions. Behind
Burleson we note standing another officer. He has no
dialogue in this scene, but will be established in this
sequence. He is the character Abbott, who works again

in scene 163 up to the end of the picture.[12] (It is up to the discretion of the director to show him in any other court scenes which are playing up to the Panama sequence.)

BURLESON (patiently):

May I remind Your Grace that our privateers have made substantial contributions to the treasury for the very purpose of providing funds for a navy?

ELIZABETH:

A large fleet is a luxury England can ill afford. You can tell your friends the Sea Hawks that I have more urgent uses for their contributions.

WOLFINGHAM (taking his cue from the queen):

Besides, there is another cost which Sir John fails to reckon. Should England attempt to vie in sea power, it may cost her the friendship of Spain.

BURLESON (less patient with Wolfingham):

I believe my lord values too highly something which doesn't exist. Have we any evidence of Philip's friendship?

WOLFINGHAM:

His forbearance when our privateers harass his commerce and plunder his possessions.

ELIZABETH:

I suspect that Philip forbears only because . . . (astutely) well, what else can he do?

BURLESON:

He can bide his time, Majesty, until his great Armada is built. Then he can strike quickly. Before we are ready.

WOLFINGHAM:

I fear Sir John has delusions of danger. Spain is a vast empire. Naturally she needs a vast fleet to defend it. The Armada is no threat to England, unless . . . by provoking Philip, we choose to make it so.

ELIZABETH:
Let me be clear, Wolfingham. My reason for refusing to build a fleet is to spare the purses of my subjects—not the feelings of Philip . . . In fact, I have some serious questions to put to his ambassador. Is Don Alvarez not due?

WOLFINGHAM:
Overdue, Your Grace. I feel some concern for his safety.

ELIZABETH (humorously):
Spanish ships are notoriously slow; he should charter an English boat.

DISSOLVE TO:

43. LONG SHOT OF THE ALBATROSS (MINIATURE) sailing along with "The Lizard" in sight.[13]

CUT TO:

44. MED. SHOT WAIST OF THE ALBATROSS
Thorpe is standing by the starboard rail of the poop deck, next to the small swivel gun. Ostensibly, Thorpe is gazing off toward the horizon. Actually, he takes occasional quick glances in a direction almost immediately below him. (In the background of Thorpe, we can see sailors busying themselves with preparation prior to landing.)

45. MED. SHOT MARIA ON THE QUARTERDECK GALLERY
of the stern (from the water level angle directly behind the ship). The quarterdeck gallery is a small balcony leading off the captain's quarters about midway up the stern. The balcony has a carved outer railing and ornamental windows on the inside wall. Directly above it is the ship's name: The Albatross of Dover. In the still higher background is the graceful lateen sail. Maria stands in the unroofed corner of the balcony, gazing off scene, unconscious that she is being observed from above.

46. MED. SHOT   WAIST OF THE SHIP   BURKE, BEN, AND BOGGS
polishing the starboard cannon. As they work they are
glancing up toward the poop deck. Obviously they are
having a private joke and enjoying it immensely.

BOGGS:
  Look at 'im, will you? As tongue-tied as a schoolboy
  . . . Always the same when 'e 'as to talk to a
  woman.

BEN:
  'Im wot's taken a fleet of Spanish ships can't trade
  words with a slip of a girl.

BURKE:
  His ship's the only thing he cares about. He hates
  the sight of bloomin' women.

BEN:
  Not the queen, he don't.

BOGGS:
  I 'ear 'Er Majesty's the only woman 'e ever could
  talk up to without 'is knees bucklin'.

BURKE:
  That's different. Man to man, I calls it.

BEN (low voice):
  That bloomin' monkey we took aboard at Venta
  Cruz . . . Did you 'ear who 'e's givin' it to? 'Er
  Majesty . . . !

BOGGS:
  I says there's two kinds of monkeys: the ones you
  find in trees, and the ones that women make outa
  sailors.

They laugh but quickly desist as evidently the captain's
glance has strayed their way. The three sailors begin to
polish harder than ever. Camera pans to Thorpe looking
closely in the direction of the three. Then he glances

down below him again. He coughs once or twice, finally
screws up the courage.

THORPE:

> Er, uh . . . your first trip to England, señorita?

47. MED. CLOSE SHOT MARIA ON THE GALLERY
She looks up with surprise in the direction of Thorpe's
voice, then quickly away from him and back toward the
rail.

MARIA:

> Yes.

Camera trucks back, includes Thorpe on the rail of the
poop deck some distance above her. We see more of the
stern and the lateen rigging of the mizzenmast. Both
Thorpe and Maria have to raise their voices slightly,
enough to preclude any suggestion of intimacy which
Maria's pride would not allow, although she is by now
slightly intrigued by the English captain. Off scene the
low strains of the chanty are still audible.[14]

THORPE (making conversation):

> They call that promontory "The Lizard"— You're
> looking at it, aren't you? It got its name from . . .

MARIA:

> Yes?

THORPE:

> I . . . I don't remember how it got its name.

The beginning of a smile appears on Maria's face (un-
seen to Thorpe, since her back is turned), but she
quickly checks it and continues to stare off scene.

THORPE (trying to draw her into conversation):

> Have you been comfortable on the ship?

MARIA:

> Yes, thank you.

THORPE:

She hasn't all the luxuries of a galleass, but she's a fine ship. I'm very proud of her.

MARIA:

Are you?

THORPE (taken aback):

Why, yes—of course. (Tries to say something amusing in his effort to please her.) You'll find the *Albatross* much safer from attack . . . Besides, you've made better time. (Camera pans up slightly to show the sail bellying in a stiff breeze, then back to Thorpe and Maria.) We have an old English proverb: "Those who sail without oars, stay on good terms with the wind." (Shyly.) You . . . you don't care to talk . . .

MARIA (turns, looks directly up at him):

Captain Thorpe, I'm not in the habit of conversing with a thief. I thought I'd made that quite clear.

THORPE (now a little angry):

All except your definition. Is a thief an *Englishman* who steals?

MARIA:

It's anyone who steals—whether it's piracy . . . or robbing women.

THORPE:

I've been admiring the jewelry we found in your chest . . . especially the wrought gold. Some of it I recognized as Aztec. I wonder just how the Indians were . . . (selecting his word with care) persuaded to part with it.

Maria gives him a furious look, turns abruptly, and disappears through the balcony door. The camera holds on Thorpe's face, which shows he is immediately contrite and would like to take back his ironic remark.

48.   MED. SHOT   MARIA'S CABIN
Actually a room in the captain's quarters, surrendered
by Thorpe. Maria comes rushing in the door, stops short
as she sees her small jewel casket waiting for her on the
table. She continues uncertainly to the table, lifts up the
carved top of the casket, and looks down.

49.   INSERT   THE JEWEL CASKET
On top of her jewels lies a note, reading as follows:
"Doña Maria . . . Only a pirate would deprive you of
these jewels . . . Francis Thorpe."

50.   MARIA
Her head moves up slightly in the direction we know
Thorpe to be, and her expression noticeably softens as
she partly revises her opinion of the English captain.

CUT TO:

51.   THORPE   STILL AT THE POOP DECK RAIL
looking off reverently toward the land. Pan to Tuttle,
Barrett, and other freed slaves, who look in the same
direction.

TUTTLE:
England . . .

CUT TO:

52.   "THE LIZARD"   (MINIATURE, MUCH CLOSER THAN NO. 43)
now quite distinct—a rocky ledge of land.

DISSOLVE TO:

53.   MED. LONG SHOT   THRONE ROOM OF PALACE   DAY
looking toward the main entrance. With the sound of
trumpets the heavy doors swing open, trumpeters take
their place on either side, and the colorful court procession begins—courtiers, knights, gentlemen pensioners,
etc. (moving toward the camera).
    The entire company, which includes Wolfingham and
Alvarez, spreads out and the queen walks majestically
to her throne as camera pans with her. Taking their

places on either side of her are eight ladies-in-waiting in purple and eight maids of honor in white. Camera rests for a moment on Maria, radiant and smiling, among the maids of honor.

54.   MED. SHOT   THE THRONE   ELIZABETH AND WOLFINGHAM
Wolfingham comes forward and bows to her.

WOLFINGHAM:
Your Grace.

ELIZABETH:
Lord Wolfingham . . .

WOLFINGHAM:
With your gracious permission, I wish to present to Your Majesty His Excellency, Don Alvarez de Córdoba, ambassador from the court of Spain.

Alvarez steps forward, bows to the queen.

ALVAREZ:
Your Majesty . . .

ELIZABETH:
Welcome to England, Your Excellency.

ALVAREZ:
Thank you, my lady . . . Before I take up certain matters with Your Grace, may I present my niece, Doña Maria.

Doña Maria comes forward with a low curtsy before the throne. Elizabeth looks at her admiringly, speaks to Alvarez.

ELIZABETH:
Your niece will grace England by her presence.

MARIA:
You are very kind, Your Majesty.

ELIZABETH (speaks a trifle wistfully):
You are very beautiful. (As Maria backs off from the queen, Elizabeth suddenly changes to a brusque vein in an evident attempt to anticipate the coming protest of the ambassador.) Don Alvarez, my lord chancellor informs me you bring new grievances from your much-aggrieved monarch, King Philip.

Alvarez, taken aback by this abrupt thrust, summons his dignity.

ALVAREZ:
There is nothing my lord and king desires more than an end to grievances between our two nations and the growth of friendship . . .

ELIZABETH:
Then it may be well for him to consider that friendship grows slowly when nurtured only by complaints.

Wolfingham, alarmed at the way the interview has opened, steps up beside Alvarez.

WOLFINGHAM:
May I suggest, Your Grace, that the misunderstandings between us and His Excellency's government arise from one source alone: the piratical acts of English privateers.

ELIZABETH:
Reprisals, Lord Wolfingham, are not piratical acts. Last year did King Philip not confiscate twelve English ships loaded with grain, in Spanish ports?

ALVAREZ (his temper rising):
Do I understand Your Grace to justify this murderous assault on my ship on the grounds of . . .

ELIZABETH (coldly interrupting):
You forget, Don Alvarez, the queen need justify nothing. (Alvarez bows.) However, I have no inten-

tion of forgetting the insult to an ambassador in my
court . . . How much treasure was there, Don Alvarez?

ALVAREZ:
Approximately thirty thousand pounds, besides the
loss of our ship.

ELIZABETH (as if calculating for a moment):
Umm . . . And where is Captain Thorpe?

WOLFINGHAM:
As soon as I was informed of the incident, Your
Grace, I took the liberty of summoning here all the
Sea Hawks now in port.

ELIZABETH (eyes her chancellor with shrewd amusement
and speaks with just a suggestion of irony):
You are very thoughtful, my lord.

Wolfingham bows, accepts the compliment on its face
value.

WOLFINGHAM:
Your Grace.

ELIZABETH (to the usher):
Admit the Sea Hawks at once.

The usher bows.

55.   MED. SHOT   ENTRANCE ON SIDE
The usher opens the door to admit the six privateering
commanders, announcing their names as they enter:

USHER:
Captain Martin Frobisher . . . Captain John Hawkins . . . Captain George Wolfe . . . Captain
Robert Stanley . . . Captain Basil Logan . . . Captain Henry La Tour . . .[15]

They are trim, fine-appearing, military men in the naval
attire of the period. They walk briskly toward the

throne, kneel before the queen. Those of the assembly whom we see in the background regard them with questioning glances. There is a slight murmur through the hall.

SEA HAWKS (ad lib):
> Your Majesty . . . Your Majesty . . . Majesty . . .

ELIZABETH:
> But where's Captain Thorpe? (The Sea Hawks look at one another.) Do you hear me? Where is Captain Thorpe?

FROBISHER:
> We haven't seen him, Your Grace.

Elizabeth looks questioningly at Wolfingham, speaks with slight sarcasm.

ELIZABETH:
> It appears he disregarded my lord chancellor's summons.

WOLFINGHAM:
> I anticipated that, Your Majesty, and dispatched a castle guard to bring him here under arrest.

ELIZABETH (looks at him keenly):
> You're very thoughtful, my lord.

WOLFINGHAM (takes the compliment on its face value, bows):
> Your Grace . . .

ELIZABETH:
> Well, Captain Hawkins?

HAWKINS:
> Any of us would willingly act as hostage to assure you of Captain Thorpe's appearance.

ELIZABETH:
> An easy pledge, Captain Hawkins, with the castle guards dispatched to bring him here under arrest.

FROBISHER:
Your Grace . . .

ELIZABETH:
Well, Captain Frobisher?

FROBISHER:
If I may speak for my associates, I feel we must share the burden of your displeasure with Captain Thorpe.

ELIZABETH:
I see. You approve of his activities!

FROBISHER (sincerely):
We share his views, Your Grace, and to the best of our ability his activities on behalf of England.

ELIZABETH (in a temper):
Then hereafter you will allow *me* to determine in what manner England may best be served.

Camera pans to Wolfingham, Alvarez, and Maria. The two men are obviously relieved by the queen's stern attitude toward the Sea Hawks. Maria is facing a window in back of the queen. Suddenly she gasps and stares at the window.

56. MED. SHOT   REAR WINDOW
partly open, with Thorpe's monkey perched on the sill. He looks curiously at the assembled crowd and then jumps down from the window into the room. There is a murmur from the assembled people. Camera pans with the monkey as he scampers over the floor. Intrigued by his image in the polished surface, he chases it across the room. There is embarrassment and confusion among the courtiers and the ladies, who are obviously startled by this breach of court decorum. They give the intruder a wide berth as he bolts for a corridor to one side and disappears from sight. (This same monkey will be established before on board the *Albatross*.)

57. MED. SHOT   THE THRONE
Elizabeth is standing. She has finally caught sight of the monkey, and she is at first too amazed to be angry.

ELIZABETH:
Who dares to . . .

USHER (interrupts in his eagerness to acquaint the queen with his message):
Captain Thorpe is here and begs an audience with Your Grace.

ELIZABETH (distracted from the monkey by this news):
Very well, have him come in.

USHER:
Yes, Your Grace.

He walks out of the shot. The camera pans over the Sea Hawks, relieved looks on their faces, then follows the usher across the room, showing court assembly in the background, Maria among them, glancing expectantly toward the side entrance. Camera holds on the door, which the usher swings open, and Captain Thorpe stands in the doorway.

USHER (announcing):
Captain Thorpe.

58. TRUCKING SHOT
Camera follows Thorpe as he passes through the assembly on his way to the throne. Obviously the entire court is impressed by this adventurous man, whose feats have become legendary. The camera rests for a moment on Maria as she stares in surprise and evident interest at Thorpe, now appearing in his official capacity and handsomely dressed.

59. MED. SHOT   IN FRONT OF THRONE

THORPE (kneels before the queen):
Your Grace.

ELIZABETH:

Captain Thorpe, why did you fail to answer my Lord Wolfingham's summons?

THORPE:

I was in the castle at the appointed time, my lady, but I . . . (breaks into a smile) I had a slight accident.

ELIZABETH:
Accident?

THORPE:
Well, perhaps not exactly an accident, but . . .

WOLFINGHAM (steps forward):
Captain Thorpe, I just dispatched a castle guard to look for you . . .

THORPE (dryly):
Yes, I had the pleasure of directing them to the ship.

WOLFINGHAM:
They had orders to bring you here under arrest!

THORPE (politely and deliberately misunderstands):
Oh, an escort was unnecessary, my lord. I know my way very well.

Wolfingham frowns. There is an amused stir through the room. Elizabeth covers a smile with her hand.

ELIZABETH:

Captain Thorpe, I have a more serious charge preferred against you. His Excellency, Don Alvarez, ambassador to this court, states that you did attack, plunder, and sink the galleass *Santa Eulalia* on which he was a passenger under the flag and protection of His Sovereign, King Philip of Spain . . . Is this charge true?

THORPE:

Partly, Your Grace, yes, a large part of it.

ELIZABETH:
Part of it? Well, what is the rest?

THORPE:
We also set free twenty Englishmen imprisoned as galley slaves on His Excellency's ship.

ALVAREZ (stepping up):
Your Majesty, these men referred to by Captain Thorpe were duly tried and sentenced to the galley by a qualified court.

THORPE:
I submit, Your Grace, that the Court of the Inquisition is not qualified to pass fair judgment upon English seamen or to subject them to the cruel indignities of the Spanish galley.

The other sea captains, who are in back of Thorpe, show their approval, but restrain themselves from any expression of it. Wolfingham takes a step forward.

WOLFINGHAM:
Your Grace, it appears that the captain wishes to justify what in plain words is a desire for plunder, with no respect for the interests of Spain.

THORPE (pointedly):
The interests of Spain do not command my respect as they evidently do His Lordship's.

WOLFINGHAM (enraged at his implication):
Your Majesty, I protest!

ELIZABETH (sharply):
Captain Thorpe, you will at least show the proper respect for my ministers.

Thorpe bows to her.

ALVAREZ:
Your Grace, I appeal to you . . .

ELIZABETH:

> One moment, Don Alvarez . . . (Turns her gaze back on Thorpe.) And so you have taken it upon yourself to remedy the defects of Spanish justice?

THORPE (nods):

> Insofar as it lies within my power.

ELIZABETH (with bitter sarcasm):

> And you conceive it to be part of your . . . mission to assault and loot the ship of an ambassador to the court. Captain Thorpe, do you imagine we are at war with Spain?

THORPE:

> Your Grace, Spain is at war with the world.

SEA HAWKS (ad lib):

> Aye . . . Aye . . . Aye, Your Majesty . . .

Elizabeth brings her hand down on the arm of her chair. The Sea Hawks immediately subside. She rises to her feet in a towering rage.

ELIZABETH:

> Enough of this! Listen to me, every one of you . . . Never again will you dare in my presence to condone your crimes under the mask of patriotism. No more of such talk, do you hear! . . . And in the future, let me warn each of you that any unwarranted attack upon the person or property of Spanish subjects will cost the guilty party his head . . . *His head!* Is that clear? . . . Now you may go . . . No, not you, Captain Thorpe . . . (Ominously.) I'm not finished with you. (Thorpe waits as the others continue off.) You will accompany the captain of the guards to my chamber, where you will wait my further pleasure.[16]

Thorpe bows. The captain of the guards steps forward. Alvarez and Wolfingham exchange looks of intense satisfaction. Thorpe falls in step beside the officer.

The camera pans with him, showing part of the assemblage watching Thorpe's exit in sympathetic silence. As he passes the maids of honor, Maria's face betrays concern. When Thorpe notices her glance, however, her expression immediately changes to bland indifference.

60.   MED. SHOT   IN FRONT OF THE THRONE   ALVAREZ, WOLFINGHAM, ELIZABETH

ELIZABETH:
Don Alvarez, you may convey my regrets to His Majesty, King Philip, and assure him that this unhappy incident will have no recurrence.

ALVAREZ (beams):
My humble thanks, Your Grace. May I also inform him that the offender in this instance will be forced to make full restitution?

ELIZABETH (rises, interrupts impatiently):
You will tell him exactly what I told you to tell him . . . nothing more.

As Alvarez steps back in disappointed silence she rises abruptly, walks down from her throne and through the assembly, who bow as she passes.

CUT TO:

61.   MED. SHOT   AN ARCHWAY IN A CORRIDOR
leading to the queen's chamber. Between the folds of a brocaded curtain that hangs from the arch, we see peeking out the wizened, inquisitive face of Thorpe's South American monkey, evidently still on the loose and a trifle bewildered by his new surroundings. Into the shot walks Thorpe and a castle guard. Joyfully the monkey leaps from his hiding place to Thorpe's shoulder. The guard looks astonished and Thorpe relieved.

THORPE:
Well! So you'll run away, will you? And make me late for my appointment . . . (Camera trucks with the guard and Thorpe as they continue through the

arch and into another corridor, with Thorpe talking to the monkey perched on his shoulder.) That was very ungrateful of you. It isn't every monkey who can live in a palace. (The monkey contritely puts his face against Thorpe's cheek.) Hereafter, mind your manners. And if your royal mistress should happen to like you, put in a good word for me. I think I shall need it.

They are now going through a doorway into the queen's chamber. Thorpe stops abruptly as he looks up to see the queen entering from the opposite corridor, also escorted by a guard.

61A.   MED. SHOT   PRIVATE CHAMBER OF THE QUEEN
This room is the royal equivalent of a private study. On one wall is a large decorated map of the New World. On the opposite wall is a low dressing table, with powder boxes and pieces of cotton; above it hangs a mirror. On a side wall is a large portrait of King Philip of Spain.

With a gesture of his head, Thorpe tosses the monkey from his shoulder and kneels on the floor in front of the queen. Her mood appears to be the same as in the throne room. She raises her eyebrows at sight of the monkey and glowers down at Thorpe. The guards who opened the doors notice Elizabeth's ominous expression. After a quick glance of sympathy toward the kneeling Thorpe and a horrified look at the monkey, they are glad to fade out of the room.

By now the monkey has observed Thorpe's attitude and mimics it. He bows his head and kneels to one side and just behind Thorpe, then grins up at the queen. This is too much for Elizabeth. Her features relax and suddenly, in remembrance of something, she breaks into a roar of laughter.

ELIZABETH:
    He looks like Wolfingham . . . the teeth, the smile—exactly . . .

Thorpe's expression is amazed and relieved. He rises, glances around at the monkey, and joins heartily in the laugh. But at this the queen abruptly sobers, and Thorpe discreetly follows suit.

THORPE (gestures toward the monkey):
My friend from Brazil was very anxious to pay his respects to Your Grace.

ELIZABETH (uncertain as to how angry she should be):
Evidently more anxious than you. He paid my court an earlier visit.

THORPE (smiles):
Oh, that's where he was? I was looking for him. That's why I was late.

ELIZABETH:
Why on earth did you bring him here?

THORPE:
I thought he might amuse my lady, and that was more than I could hope to do.

Elizabeth is obviously intrigued by the monkey, now perched on a chest at one side of the room. As she approaches the animal he looks at Thorpe for a cue, then in desperation quickly doffs his hat to the queen, who melts at the gesture. She addresses the monkey.

ELIZABETH:
You're a rascal . . . (with a gesture of her head toward Thorpe) like your former master . . . But I'm fond of rascals—some of them.

The camera pulls back to a wider angle revealing five large chests with heavy iron bands and hinges.

ELIZABETH (as she catches sight of the chests):
Well, I see you've had a profitable voyage.

By now Thorpe fully realizes what he suspected before: that the queen's great show of displeasure in the previous scene was for the benefit of the Spanish ambassador. We see that there is a complete understanding between Thorpe and the queen, although it is also evident that no one can ever be certain of permanent favor with this shrewd and capricious monarch.

Thorpe crosses to the nearest chest, raises the lid, and takes out a small jewel case. He opens it and holds it out to the queen, whose eyes light with pleasure.

ELIZABETH:

Captain Thorpe!

THORPE:

For you, my lady.

Elizabeth lifts out of the box a silver pendant with a single large pearl and holds it up before her in sheer feminine delight.

ELIZABETH:

See the light in it! . . . A West Indian pearl, is it not?

THORPE:

Yes, madam. By some mischance it was on its way to Spain when I . . . diverted it. (Smiles, trying to skip lightly over a tender subject. He looks at portrait of Philip of Spain on wall.) Er . . . you might say I came between Philip and the oyster.

ELIZABETH (obviously more interested in the pearl than in her good-humored reprimand; slips the pendant around her neck as she speaks):

Captain Thorpe, I fear Wolfingham is right. You are an incorrigible pirate.

She turns her back to Thorpe so that he can fasten the clasp on her neck.

THORPE:

Your Grace, I have a conscience about pearls. They should be worn only by one whose throat matches their own luster.

ELIZABETH (coyly pleased, but chiding him):
And have you any other scruples?

THORPE (sincerely):
One. Never willfully to displease Your Majesty.

ELIZABETH (smiles enigmatically):
Have you?

THORPE (looks at her closely, smiles):
I trust not . . . but one can be mistaken.

ELIZABETH (goes to the mirror, admires the pearl on her neck as she talks):
Well, I should not advise you to make a practice of . . . diverting Spanish ambassadors.

THORPE:
Your Grace, the ambassador's galleass was propelled by English oars. I merely substituted English sails.

ELIZABETH (the queen again; speaks directly):
Captain Thorpe, we have moral rights on our side; Spain has the law on hers. Bear that in mind in your future ventures. (Thorpe bows.) Now to business.

THORPE (takes a paper from his pocket, hands it to the queen):
An inventory of the treasure, Your Majesty, with the crown's share (indicating the chests) at your disposal.

ELIZABETH (glances over the paper, her eyes gleaming):
Excellent. I shall put it to good use.

THORPE (cautiously):
If what I have done has pleased Your Grace, I have a favor to ask . . .

ELIZABETH (suspiciously):
Well?

THORPE:

That our contributions will induce Your Majesty to begin work on the fleet.

ELIZABETH (immediately flares up):

Fleet! Must I listen to that from you, too?

THORPE:

But the Armada, Your Grace . . .

ELIZABETH:

Are you so sure Philip will attack?

THORPE:

Have we any assurance that he won't?

The queen walks thoughtfully across the room, then turns to Thorpe, her temper subdued.

ELIZABETH:

Captain Thorpe, with all the contributions of the Sea Hawks, we cannot possibly match Philip's vast resources. Our safety lies in diplomacy, not force.

THORPE:

Your Majesty, suppose Philip's resources, or at least a large portion of them, were not to reach them . . . (smiles) were to be diverted?

ELIZABETH:

Just what is going on in that piratical mind of yours?

THORPE:

Your Grace, the lifeblood of Spain is its New World treasure. Within three months a year's plunder of gold from Mexico and Peru leaves Panama bound for Spain. With ten of our best privateering ships . . .

ELIZABETH (breaks in):

No! I forbid it! A concerted attack on the gold fleet would be regarded by Philip as an overt act of war . . . which even I could not explain away.

THORPE:
>Very well. Let it be a private venture . . . one ship—the *Albatross*—and a picked crew.

ELIZABETH:
>Impossible . . . the Spanish convoy would overwhelm you. (She sits in front of a small table.)

THORPE:
>On the sea, yes . . . (He crosses eagerly to the New World map on the far wall.)

62. CLOSE SHOT THORPE AT THE MAP

THORPE:
>but I have another plan, Your Majesty. The treasure crosses Panama by mule caravan here . . .

63. MED. CLOSE SHOT ELIZABETH
watching Thorpe intently, her fingers drumming on the table.

THORPE'S VOICE (over scene):
>. . . from the west coast to the Caribbean—a distance of sixty leagues.

64. MED. SHOT THORPE AND ELIZABETH

THORPE:
>Now between Nombre de Dios and Panama City—this strip here—is jungle so dense that a small force could attack from ambush.[17]

As Thorpe turns around from the map the camera pans with Elizabeth as she walks thoughtfully to the small table on the opposite side of the room, apparently weighing her decision. In a preoccupied manner, she takes up a piece of cotton from the table and begins to powder her face in front of the mirror.

65. MED. CLOSE SHOT   ELIZABETH AT THE MIRROR
Elizabeth powdering her face. In the background is the
monkey, watching her curiously from his perch. The
camera pans up close to the mirror, where we see the
reflection of Thorpe, who is waiting intently for the
queen's reply. Elizabeth puts down the cotton and
powder and turns slowly from her vanity table. As she
walks out of the shot the camera holds on the spot, and
we see the monkey jump down from his perch to the
vanity table. He picks up a piece of cotton in his hand,
looks at it curiously.

66.   MED. SHOT   ELIZABETH AND THORPE   IN FRONT OF THE
MAP

ELIZABETH:
Could such a plan possibly succeed?

THORPE:
It would have one chance of success . . . if the
Spanish were taken by complete surprise . . . Your
Majesty, have I your permission to try?

ELIZABETH (shrewdly, after a moment's reflection):
Captain Thorpe, if you undertook such a venture
you would do so without the approval of the Queen
of England . . . (Her expression softens.) However, you would take with you the grateful affection
of Elizabeth.

THORPE:
My lady, then I shall take with me what I prize
above all things. (He leans to her hand and kisses it
reverently, then turns and goes out.)

67.   CLOSE SHOT   ELIZABETH
Unconsciously she fondles the pearl that hangs from her
neck as she stands looking after him. Both her feminine
vanity and her queenly pride have been gracefully
complimented. But suddenly, as she turns partly

around, her elated expression is transformed to horrified wrath.

68.   CLOSE SHOT   THE MONKEY
      looking mischievously up at his mistress with a face as powdered as hers, still whisking the cotton across his features in an exact mimicry of the queen.

                                              DISSOLVE TO:

69.   MED. SHOT   A PALACE GARDEN   DAY
      MARIA AND MISS LATHAM
      Maria and Miss Latham are cutting roses. Actually Maria is furtively watching for Thorpe when he comes out from his interview with Elizabeth. She deliberates a long time before cutting each blossom, but even so the bouquet is growing to alarming proportions. As she cuts a flower Maria hands it to Miss Latham, who holds the large, thorny bouquet gingerly at arm's length.

MISS LATHAM (with good-natured irony):
      Don't you think, my dear, we could manage with what we have?

MARIA (looking hopefully up the walk that leads from the corridor):
      No, I want a few more . . . (Miss Latham follows Maria's glance and holds the flowers resignedly.) Look, Martha, don't you think this one is pretty?

MISS LATHAM:
      Very pretty—you've quite a lot just like it.

MARIA:
      No, this is a different species . . . It's a little darker, you see . . .

MISS LATHAM (significantly):
      Oh, I see . . .

MARIA (resenting the inference):
      Martha, what are you thinking about?

MISS LATHAM (rattles on innocently):
> Oh, I was just thinking about our voyage. I must
> say, I prefer English boats to Spanish. There's more
> air on them. (As she spies Thorpe coming toward
> them.) You must excuse me, my dear. Here, you'd
> better take these.

Before Maria can object, Miss Latham thrusts the
bouquet in her arms and beats a hasty retreat, in the
opposite direction from which Thorpe is coming. Maria
struggles with the unwieldy bouquet. In her confusion
she pricks her finger on a thorn and drops the bouquet
to the ground as Thorpe comes into the scene.

70.   TWO-SHOT   MARIA AND THORPE
Thorpe stops in surprise. Maria, angry with herself,
puts the pricked finger to her mouth.

THORPE:
> May I help you? (He bends down to gather up the
> immense quantity of roses. He tries to find some-
> thing to say.) You . . . you must be very fond of
> English roses.

MARIA:
> My mother told me of your rose gardens. She was
> an Englishwoman.

THORPE (glancing up):
> Oh, that explains a good deal . . .

MARIA (unwilling to be so easily understood):
> But I prefer the Spanish iris.

THORPE (amused):
> Naturally—it has no thorns.

MARIA (screws up her courage):
> Captain Thorpe . . .

THORPE:
> Yes?

He continues bending over the flowers, but only pretends to gather them as he weighs the import of her words.

MARIA:

> I didn't get a chance on the boat—I want to thank you for returning my jewels . . . I'm sorry for what I said about robbing women. And if you think it would help I'd be glad to speak to the queen . . . tell her how kindly you treated us . . . that we don't want you to be punished.

THORPE (amused by this last, but also moved by the girl's pride-swallowing, which obviously costs her a great effort):

> Oh, I . . . think I can stand the punishment. (He straightens up, speaks earnestly as he looks in her face.) But I'm very grateful for your concern. Perhaps you can guess what it means to me.

MARIA (pretending):

> I'm afraid I . . . haven't any notion.

THORPE (speaks sincerely):

> When I first saw you, I thought you were a marble statue, beautifully wrought. Then I watched your face when you saw the slaves, and the marble came to life . . . I knew one day you'd forgive me.

MARIA:

> Captain Thorpe, I have forgiven you, but— (She stops, unable to go on.)

THORPE:

> Doña Maria, is forgiveness . . . all you feel?

MARIA:

> Have I led you to believe there was anything else?

THORPE:

> Not from what you've said . . . just something I thought I saw in your eyes.

MARIA (without raising her eyes):
> You're mistaken.

THORPE:
> I'm sorry.

Maria raises her head and looks full at him, her dark eyes proudly concealing her feeling. Thorpe looks at her for a moment, then pretends to be convinced. He bends down and gathers up the rest of her roses.

THORPE (watching her out of the corner of his eye):
> I guess it's just as well . . . since I'm going back to sea.

MARIA (for a moment betrays herself):
> What! . . . Oh . . .

THORPE:
> And I shall be away for a long time.

MARIA:
> You . . . you're leaving soon?

THORPE:
> As soon as the *Albatross* is ready . . . within a fortnight.

He rises, hands her the bouquet, now assembled. She looks at him helplessly, torn between pride and her desire.

THORPE (speaks very simply):
> The roses look . . . different when you hold them. (He pauses for a moment, hoping she will reveal her feeling, then continues to cover the pause.) Doña Maria, in the garden of a convent in Peru there's a beautiful statue. The Spanish nuns call it Nuestra Señora del Rosario . . . This is how I'll remember you . . . as my lady of the roses.

He leaves her quickly and she stands wretchedly looking after him with the flowers in her arms.[18]

DISSOLVE TO:

71. FULL SHOT   MAIN DECK OF THE ALBATROSS   DAY
in its dock at Dover, with part of the wharf visible on one side of the deck. A scene of bustling activity in preparation for the voyage. A steady stream of supplies: food, barrels of ale, powder, cannonballs, etc., are pouring over the rail of the *Albatross*. Below on the dock we see supplies being unloaded from mule carts.

72. MED. SHOT   MAIN DECK OF THE SHIP
Carl is supervising the loading.

CARL:
> Down in the hold with that, Burke . . . Careful with that powder . . . Move along, men, or we'll be here till Saint Thomas's Day.

A stranger, later identified as Kroner, walks up to Carl.

KRONER:
> A long voyage, eh, mate?

CARL (ironically):
> No, we're just loading 'er to the gills for ballast.

KRONER (passing over the remark):
> Goin' to do some trading, I suppose?

CARL:
> See those cannonballs, mister? Where we go, we trade 'em lead for gold at even weights . . . If you're here to sign on, stranger, the captain's in his quarters . . . through that door.

He turns away. Kroner walks toward the door indicated.

73. MED. SHOT   THE CAPTAIN'S ROOM
(NOTE: Same room previously occupied by Maria.) Thorpe is seated at his table with paper and quill. William Tuttle, one of the freed slaves, stands on the opposite side of the table. Behind Tuttle is Eli Matson, look-

ing sheepish and woebegone. From off scene continues
the sound of loading.

THORPE (kindly):
I thought you might not want to go back to the sea
so soon, Tuttle.

TUTTLE (simply):
I'm a sailor, Captain.

THORPE:
And a right good one. Just the kind we need on this
trip. Report to the bos'n in the morning.

TUTTLE:
Aye, sire.

As he goes out Eli moves up to the table, fidgeting nervously with his hat in his hands.

ELI:
Cap'n . . .

THORPE:
Well, Matson?

ELI:
Cap'n, if you don't mind my askin', I suppose after
wot I done, there ain't no place for me on the *Albatross*.

THORPE (his stern manner gradually relaxes):
There's always a place for a brave man, Eli . . .
(Dryly.) Especially one who's learned to obey or-
ders.

ELI (grasps Thorpe's hand, pumps it energetically):
Cap'n, there ain't no man on earth I'd rather serve.
And I'll make it up to ye. Thank you, sir, thank you.

Eli is almost weeping. He starts to go, then remembers
his hat, grabs it, and rushes out. Thorpe watches his exit
with amusement.

THORPE (calls as he makes entries on his paper):
  Next! (Kroner steps into the room, stands in front of
  the table. Thorpe glances up at him casually, then
  asks routine questions, filling the answers in a
  blank.) Name . . .

KRONER:
  Kroner, Captain . . . Samuel Kroner, seaman, first
  class.

THORPE:
  Age?

KRONER:
  Forty-two.

THORPE:
  Last ship?

KRONER:
  The *Dorsey.*

THORPE:
  Your papers?

KRONER:
  I didn't bring them, Captain. I wasn't ready to sign
  until I knew where we're shipping.

THORPE (for the first time scrutinizes him closely):
  Oh, you weren't . . .

KRONER:
  Don't a man have a right to know what he's signin'
  on for, Captain?

THORPE:
  My men are willing to follow me wherever I take
  them . . . (significantly) without any questions
  . . . Get off the ship.

Kroner rises quickly, turns toward the door as we

                                            DISSOLVE TO:

74. MED. SHOT   WOLFINGHAM'S STUDY   KRONER,
WOLFINGHAM, ALVAREZ
Kroner, now recognized as a spy, is making his report.

KRONER:
> . . . and I says to myself, this ain't the usual
> preparations. This here voyage is something dif-
> ferent. But that's all I could find out, Your Lord-
> ship. Not a man in his crew what knows where he's
> goin'.

Wolfingham and Alvarez exchange glances.

WOLFINGHAM:
> Kroner, Thorpe's destination is of vital concern.
> You will have him watched from now until the day
> he sails. The money will be placed at your disposal
> by my steward.

KRONER:
> Very good, Your Lordship. (Bows and goes out.)

ALVAREZ (after the door closes, speaks indignantly):
> Then this Thorpe is free again to plunder where he
> chooses . . . in spite of the queen.

WOLFINGHAM (shrewdly):
> Or perhaps *for* the queen. Hereafter we shall do
> better to rely on our own devices than the assur-
> ances of a clever woman.

ALVAREZ (studies Wolfingham keenly, with a slight trace
of suspicion):
> But surely she would not neglect to inform her lord
> chancellor of the nature of such an important voy-
> age.

WOLFINGHAM (aware of the ambassador's suspicions of a
possible doublecross):
> Her Grace did inform me that Thorpe was un-
> dertaking a trading expedition up the Nile. (Wryly.)
> I pretended to believe her . . . Does that reassure
> Your Excellency?

ALVAREZ:
Forgive me, my lord, if any suspicion crossed my mind. His Majesty, King Philip, has implicit confidence in your loyalty to his interests.

WOLFINGHAM:
His Gracious Majesty and I have an interest in common . . . a ruler friendly to Spain on England's throne.

ALVAREZ (shrewdly):
Like . . . you, Lord Wolfingham.

WOLFINGHAM (nods):
Don Alvarez, we serve others best when at the same time we serve ourselves.[19]

They smile at each other with complete understanding.

DISSOLVE TO:

75.   INT. CHARTMAKER'S SHOP   LONDON   DAY
It is a small, musty shop, cluttered with mariners' instruments and nautical charts. On shelves and tables are quadrants, globes, astrolabes, crossjacks, hourglasses, half-hour glasses and parchment logbooks. On the walls are large parchment maps, elaborately colored and decorated. Under a window in the back corner is the chartmaker's worktable, with paper and rulers and quills and half-finished work. The chartmaker, an aged little man, whitehaired and nearsighted, an ex-seaman and amateur astronomer, is talking animatedly to Thorpe, agog with the honor of being commissioned by the great sea captain.

CHARTMAKER:
Aye, Captain, you can count on me . . . I'm the man can turn out your chart—by Wednesday certain . . .

THORPE:
You have enough information on those waters?

CHARTMAKER:
> Every bay and inlet for harboring a ship—with soundings accurate and not a reef missing.

THORPE:
> Good. That's just what I want. I'll send for it Wednesday then. (He starts out. Just as he gets to the door, Thorpe pauses, turns around. As he speaks we see through the little front display window of the shop a man standing with bent head, apparently examining something there.) I don't want any printing on the map—don't name the places.

CHARTMAKER:
> No names . . . very good, Captain. Good day, Captain Thorpe.

THORPE:
> Good day, sir.

He opens the door, goes out. As he does so the man outside lifts his head, turns around so as not to be seen by Thorpe in the street. The man is obviously one of Kroner's spies who is shadowing Thorpe.

> DISSOLVE TO:

76. INSERT
The word *Albatross* drawn in fancy scroll. A hand is just putting the final flourishes on it with a paintbrush.

> CUT TO:

77. MED. CLOSE SHOT   THE CHARTMAKER
seated at his worktable, with a map before him, the fancy lettering in the upper left-hand corner. On his face, as he looks at it, are written pride and satisfaction.

> CUT TO:

78. MED. SHOT   THE SHOP
The doorbell tinkles and the chartmaker puts down his brush, goes to the door. He admits Alvarez and

Wolfingham, who glance around the shop curiously as they enter.

CHARTMAKER (squinting at them):
How do you do, gentlemen . . .

WOLFINGHAM:
Are you the chartmaker?

CHARTMAKER:
At your service . . .

WOLFINGHAM:
I am Lord Wolfingham. This is His Imperial Majesty's ambassador, Don Alvarez de Córdoba.

CHARTMAKER (bowing):
I am honored, Your Excellency, and my lord . . .

WOLFINGHAM:
I have been boasting to His Excellency about English chartmaking. I am anxious for him to see samples of your work . . . perhaps some charts you are in the process of making.

CHARTMAKER:
Certainly, sir . . . won't you come over by the window . . . The light's better. I'll bring them to you. (He indicates a chair in front of the worktable.) Would His Excellency prefer to see navigation charts or maps?

ALVAREZ:
The charts, if you please. My government may wish to compare them with their own.

CHARTMAKER:
Very good, sir.

As the chartmaker moves off, Alvarez takes the chair; Wolfingham stands in back of him, looking over his shoulder. At about the same moment both men see the chart on the worktable with the name Albatross in the corner.

79. INSERT   THE CHART
fastened at the corners to the wooden workboard. It is
about twenty-four by thirty inches and is printed from a
steel engraving on cloth-backed parchment. It shows a
strip of land with water on either side. Along one
coastline the water is covered with numbers, spaced
about every half inch, indicating the ocean depth at
these points. (This map shows the Panama section, but
in the absence of any names it is not recognizable as
such.) At the top of the chart is an ornamental represen-
tation of the constellation Orion. A thin line connecting
the stars in the constellation clearly outlines the figure of
the hunter, his belt, and dagger. From the tip of his
dagger a dotted line carries down to a point on the map
later identified as the Spanish treasure terminal in
Panama.

CUT TO:

80. CLOSE SHOT   ALVAREZ AND WOLFINGHAM
at the worktable, looking from the map to each other.
Alvarez gives a slight shrug indicating that he can't tell
what the map represents. Wolfingham's puzzled frown
gives way to his usual bland expression as the
chartmaker returns with several rolled-up parchments
in his hand.

WOLFINGHAM (indicating Thorpe's chart):
This is very interesting . . .

CHARTMAKER:
I just finished that one as you gentlemen came in.
(He spreads out another chart on top of it.) This
one's a section of the west coast of Africa. You will
see it's worked out with such detail that a navigator
can sail his ship through waters unknown to him
. . .

ALVAREZ:
Yes, indeed . . . excellent work.

He starts to lift it up to get back to Thorpe's chart underneath, but just as he does so, the chartmaker spreads out another one on top of them both.

CHARTMAKER:
> Here are some straits . . . tricky to navigate and, if I may say so, tricky to chart.

WOLFINGHAM:
> What do the figures of the constellations signify on the top of the map?

CHARTMAKER:
> Purely a decoration, my lord. I take the constellation that has its zenith over the charted territory . . . every seaman knows them . . . like the Southern Cross over these Straits of Magellan . . . (Smiles.) Merely a conceit of mine, so people will recognize my work.

ALVAREZ:
> Quite an original idea. (He removes the two charts on top to uncover the *Albatross*'s.) This figure with the dagger pointing down is Orion the hunter is it not?

CHARTMAKER:
> Yes, Your Excellency. (Regarding Alvarez with just a trace of suspicion.) Then Your Excellency has some knowledge of astronomy?

ALVAREZ (to throw him off):
> Not as much as I should like to have. (In light vein.) They say that even our fortunes rest with the stars.
>> DISSOLVE TO:

81. MED. CLOSE SHOT CORNER OF A LIBRARY
where some books and charts are visible. The court astronomer, a quaint-looking, scholarly man in a skullcap and a long robe, stands at a globe of the then known world, as he instructs Alvarez and Wolfingham, who listen intently.

ASTRONOMER:

You see, gentlemen, the orbit of Orion is approximately this narrow path between the equator and the ten-degree parallel. The constellation appears to move overhead as the earth turns on its axis. Obviously, the section of land you are seeking must be somewhere on this belt.

82.   CLOSE SHOT   THE GLOBE
slowly revolving, with two fingers of the astronomer forming the two edges of Orion's orbit as it is described on the earth.

ASTRONOMER'S VOICE (over scene):

From your memory of the chart, it appears the strip is too long to be an island, not large enough to be a continent.

The fingers pass over the continent of Africa at this point, then continue over the Atlantic Ocean.

ASTRONOMER'S VOICE (continuing over scene):

Therefore we may deduce it is an isthmus. The only isthmus running east and west under Orion's orbit is this connecting link between the two continents of the New World.

As he says this the globe comes to a stop with the Isthmus of Panama stretched between the two fingers.

83.   MED. CLOSE SHOT   ASTRONOMER, ALVAREZ, WOLFINGHAM
at the globe.

ASTRONOMER (with scholarly pride):

Gentlemen, here is your charted strip of land . . . the Isthmus of Panama.

DISSOLVE TO:

84.   MED. SHOT   THORPE'S CABIN ON THE ALBATROSS
Thorpe is seated at his desk. Carl enters with a rolled parchment, which he hands to the captain.

CARL:
From the chartmaker, Captain.

THORPE:
Thanks, Mr. Pitt. (He unrolls the chart, gives it a quick glance.) Very good . . . I think I'll go to London before we sail. You'll take charge here and finish the loading.

CARL (grins):
Aye, Cap'n . . . More business in London?

THORPE:
Yes, I have some things to . . . What are you grinning about?

CARL (quickly sobers):
Nothing . . . I wasn't grinning—not me.

THORPE (sees the humor, grins himself):
Carl, I *have* an appointment with someone. (Wryly.) However, she doesn't know it yet.

Carl can enjoy his grin openly now. He goes out the door.

BURLESON'S VOICE (off scene):
Hello, Carl. Captain Thorpe in his cabin?

CARL'S VOICE (off scene):
Sure he is. Go right in, Sir John.

Burleson enters. Thorpe stands to greet him.

THORPE:
Sir John . . . I'm glad to see you.

They shake hands cordially. There is a fatherly attitude in Burleson's evident fondness for the younger man.

BURLESON:
You're looking trim, Francis. Like your ship.

THORPE:
> We sail next week, Sir John. I was just going into London . . . a farewell visit.

BURLESON:
> Sailing next week, you say. That's what I came to see you about . . . You couldn't be ready sooner, could you?

THORPE:
> Why, yes—I suppose so—if there's some reason . . .

BURLESON:
> There is, Francis. A good reason. (In a lower voice.) I bring you a message from the queen. She wishes you to set sail at the earliest possible moment. It appears that some members of her court are asking too many questions about your . . . (wryly) trading expedition up the Nile.

THORPE (obviously disappointed, but making the best of it):
> I see . . . Very well, Sir John, I'll not go to London. You can inform Her Majesty we'll sail with tomorrow's tide.

BURLESON (puts a hand on Thorpe's arm):
> And with my blessing, Francis . . . wherever you may be going.[20]

DISSOLVE TO:

85.   TWO-SHOT   THE AMBASSADOR'S APARTMENT   ALVAREZ, MARIA
facing each other across a small table on which is a chessboard, the pieces distributed as in the middle of an evenly matched game. Alvarez studies the board. He is humming a Spanish tune.

MARIA:
> You're feeling very happy, Uncle?

ALVAREZ:
What? . . . Oh, yes, yes.

MARIA:
You've had good news?

ALVAREZ:
Excellent news . . . Let's see, if I castle, I'll lose this pawn . . .

MARIA (curious):
Is it a secret?

ALVAREZ:
You wouldn't be interested, my dear.

Miss Latham opens the door.

MISS LATHAM:
Mr. Kroner to see you, Don Alvarez.

ALVAREZ:
Have him come in, Miss Latham.

MISS LATHAM (speaks off scene):
Come in, please.

KRONER (as he enters):
Thank you. (He remains at the doorway, nods to Alvarez and Maria.) Your Excellency . . . señorita . . .

Alvarez rises. Maria smiles, remains at the table.

ALVAREZ:
You have news from my lord?

KRONER:
Aye, the best possible news. Captain López sailed this morning. He'll get to Panama before Captain Thorpe.

Maria looks up, startled, then quickly down toward the chessboard.

ALVAREZ:
Please congratulate his lordship, and convey my
best wishes.

KRONER:
Thank you, señor.

He brings his heels together, bows, and goes off. Alvarez walks back to his seat at the table.

ALVAREZ:
Well, the English pirate has plundered his last ship.

MARIA (keeps her eyes on the board):
Uncle, what will they do to him?

ALVAREZ:
Piracy is punishable with death . . . or, if Spain is
disposed to be lenient, there's the galley.

Maria suddenly moves one of her chessmen.

ALVAREZ (surprised at the move):
Why, Maria, what a foolish move. Look, now I can
get your knight, and that leaves the queen unpro-
tected.[21]

He begins to make the move as we

DISSOLVE TO:

86.   MARIA'S BED CHAMBER   DUSK
We discover a floor shot of Maria's feet pacing slowly up
and down, and truck back to reveal her in her bedroom,
walking distractedly up and down past the window in
an agony of indecision, and then stops at the window
staring out. And as she looks out she realizes that no
matter what her loyalties, she loves Thorpe, and she
must warn him. She hurriedly crosses toward door.

87.   TOWARD DOOR   MED. CLOSE
as she opens door and calls.

MARIA:
Martha!

She hurries across and starts putting on a cloak and bonnet as Miss Latham comes in.

MISS LATHAM:
Yes, my dear?

MARIA:
Martha, I'm going to Dover, right away.

MISS LATHAM (not batting an eyelash):
I'll order a carriage—with fast horses.

She quickly exits. Maria hurriedly finishes putting her things on.

DISSOLVE TO:

88.　PRIVATE GATEWAY　NARROW STREET　　　DUSK
MED. CLOSE PAN SHOT
A closed carriage with two spirited horses is waiting, Miss Latham talking to the driver. Maria hurries through the small private gateway.

MARIA:
Can you reach Dover tonight?

DRIVER:
With change of horses—yes, my lady.

MARIA (urgently):
As quickly as you can . . . please! (To Miss Latham.) Not a word to my uncle.

Miss Latham answers as Maria climbs in the carriage.

MISS LATHAM:
Don't worry about that . . . my dear . . . and if you see that big ruffian, Carl, give him my felicitations. (Maria smiles knowingly.) Not that he'll know what it means.

The door slams, the horses lunge at their traces, and camera pans with carriage as it speeds off scene into the dust.

DISSOLVE TO:

89. ROAD   CLOSE TRAVEL SHOT   NIGHT
of the hooves of the original horses (dark in color) thundering along the road at a mad pace over dirt road.

DISSOLVE TO:

90. ROAD   CLOSE TRAVEL SHOT   NIGHT
of the hooves of a team of white horses thundering along the road.

DISSOLVE TO:

91. MARIA   CLOSE SHOT
sitting, tired, strained and silent, in the darkness of the swaying carriage, her eyes looking unseeingly into the darkness outside.

DISSOLVE TO:

92. STREET   CLOSE TRAVEL SHOT   NIGHT
of a third change of horses, their hooves beating a mad tattoo on the cobblestones of a street.

93. STREET   NEAR DOCKS   FULL SHOT   NIGHT
as the carriage rushes down the silent, sleeping street.

94. DOCK   MED. CLOSE
The street corner onto dock that we have established as being opposite Thorpe's ship. Camera's back is to ship. The carriage comes into scene, the horses sliding to a stop in foreground. The door flies open and Maria starts to climb swiftly out, but slows down as she steps to the ground, all the eager hope fading from her face—staring strickenly off scene.

95. DOCK EDGE AND WATER   HER ANGLE
The place where Thorpe's ship was docked is empty—a few frayed rope ends and scattering of broken boxes and crates along the edge of the wharf.

96. MARIA   CLOSE SHOT
As she continues to stare, from off scene comes the voice of a town crier.

CRIER'S VOICE:
Four o'clock—and all's well.

Maria turns slowly to look.

97. CRIER   HER ANGLE
of the crier (or lamplighter) coming along the dock, carrying a lantern.

98. AT CARRIAGE   MED. CLOSE
as Maria turns and hurries off scene to him.

99. AT CRIER   MED. CLOSE
as she hurries in and stops him.

MARIA:
Where is the *Albatross?*

CRIER:
She sailed this evening on the ebb tide. (Seeing her distress.) Can I help you, my lady?

MARIA (slowly):
No . . . No—thank you.

The man bows courteously and goes on, leaving Maria staring off across the water into the misty darkness.

DISSOLVE TO:

100. STERN OF ALBATROSS   QUARTERDECK   FROM OUTSIDE
RAIL   MED. CLOSE   NIGHT
as it sails through the darkness. A dim light burns near the wheel. In foreground, leaning on the stern rail, Thorpe is staring back toward Dover, and there is a sadness in his eyes. He remains immovable for a moment, deep in thought.[22] From the distance comes a voice:

SAILOR'S VOICE:
Land's End off the starboard.

Thorpe straightens slowly from the rail and seems, in the reluctance of his turn, to say farewell to Maria.

101.　QUARTERDECK　MED. SHOT

THORPE (as he turns he calls off scene):
Ready to tack.

VOICE:
Aye, aye, Captain.

THORPE (barking orders up):
Break out topsails . . . clear the fore-to'gallant yards.

DISTANT VOICE:
Break out topsails . . . clear fore-to'gallant yards.

THORPE:
Sou'west by west, there below!

VOICE BELOW:
Sou'west by west.

Thorpe doesn't look back toward Dover again. His eyes are looking gravely into the darkness ahead. Music wells up (which will continue through the montage), and as it grows stronger, we

DISSOLVE TO:

102.　ALBATROSS ON OCEAN

The *Albatross*, under full sail, heading westward. The ship becomes a drawing which moves over a crude period map, past the Azores, over the Atlantic, into the Caribbean Sea. The map at this point merges into Thorpe's chart (seen in the chartmaker's shop) as the *Albatross* approaches Panama, finally entering an inlet where Orion's dagger is poised directly over the ship.

DISSOLVE TO:

103. FULL SHOT   PANAMA INLET   (MINIATURE)   DAYBREAK
The *Albatross* comes into the inlet. She is indistinctly
seen in the half-light before dawn. The only sounds
audible are the swish of the oars and the chatter of
tropical birds from the jungle that stretches close to the
water's edge.

CUT TO:

104. PAN SHOT   FRINGE OF JUNGLE
Camera pans up through the trees to show a bright-
plumaged bird startled into flight. Camera pans down to
the matted floor of the jungle where we catch a brief
glimpse of a dark figure peering through the trees toward the ocean. The native suddenly turns and
disappears into the dense forest.

105. MED. LONG SHOT   NATIVE
running at top speed along a trail cut through the jungle
(later identified as the mule-caravan track). He runs
from right to left.

DISSOLVE TO:

106. FULL SHOT   THE MARKETPLACE   DAY
of Venta Cruz, an inland Panama town—the halfway
house between Panama City (on the Pacific coast of the
Isthmus), where the treasure is brought from South
America, and Nombre de Dios (on the Caribbean coast),
where the Spanish ships wait to transport it to Spain.

The tropical sun is so oppressive in this section that all
activity is usually suspended during the daytime. The
mule caravans travel at night, and now at midday the
marketplace is full of dozing beasts, with great panniers
across their backs, which silent natives are loading with
gold from the treasure-house nearby. The bronze bodies
of the slaves glisten with perspiration; on their faces is
an expression of hopeless resignation. The heat is so
intense that it has arrested all motion but the trancelike
movement of the natives to and from the treasure-

house, and all sound but the occasional deep, musical sound of one of the bells around the necks of the mules.

107.   MED. SHOT   AT BUILDING
In the shade of the treasure-house doorway, leaning against the wall, we see a Spanish officer; his eyes travel over the marketplace, but he doesn't move or speak. Camera pans to show several Spanish soldiers (part of the convoy) sitting in the shade of palm trees, also watching the loading through half-closed eyes.

108.   FULL SHOT   MARKETPLACE
Suddenly the native runner (seen in the jungle) appears in the marketplace and makes straight for the officer in the doorway (the native still running in direction from right to left).

109.   MED. SHOT   AT BUILDING
The native is reeling from heat and exhaustion, gasps out an excited message in Indian dialect. The face of the officer undergoes not the slightest change of expression. He pushes himself slowly from the wall, goes to the door. Just as he opens it the native says something else to him, holding out his empty hands. The officer pauses, reaches deliberately into his money pouch, and, without turning around, tosses a coin at the native's feet, disappears into the building.
(It is suggested that throughout this tropical sequence Spanish cruelty and decadence manifest themselves in a more passive and sinister form than in the galley scenes. Instead of active brutality, emphasis should be placed on the effete cunning of the Spaniards and the spiritless submission of the natives.)

110.   MED. SHOT   OFFICE OF SPANISH COMMANDER
inside the treasure-house. General Aguerra, dressed in an impeccable uniform, is seated in a chair at his desk, reading some dispatches as he fans himself with a large

palmetto fan. Lieutenant Ortega, the officer we saw outside, enters, salutes. The general looks up but doesn't bother to return the salute.

ORTEGA:
Thorpe has arrived, señor. An inlet ten miles west of Nombre de Dios . . .

AGUERRA (with only mild interest; his fan stops for a moment):
So for once they sent me an accurate report. And on time!

ORTEGA:
Your orders, General?

AGUERRA (still musing as he continues to fan):
A long time we have waited for this meeting. A long time. (Smiles ominously as he regards the waiting officer.) Lieutenant Ortega, we must give Captain Thorpe a . . . fitting reception. You will summon all garrison officers between here and Panama City.

ORTEGA:
Very well, señor. And the treasure train?

AGUERRA:
You will leave with a small escort for Nombre de Dios at sundown as scheduled.

ORTEGA:
But the English will attack . . .

AGUERRA (interrupts him with a wave of the hand):
And you will offer no resistance . . . Captain Thorpe came a long way for the gold. We must not disappoint him. (He smiles as Ortega looks mystified.) Lieutenant, you have seen the jungle orchid. It is an attractive flower that holds out its yellow pollen. But once an insect is lured within its petals . . . (illustrating with his fingers) they close—like this.

135

The officer smiles back. The general continues to fan himself as we

DISSOLVE TO:

111. MED. SHOT   SECTION OF MULE TRACK
through the jungle. It is late afternoon now and the jungle is dark and forbidding on either side of the track. Thorpe and twenty of his men (all but those left aboard the *Albatross*) are gathered around Oliver Scott, who has just returned from a scouting expedition. The voices of all are low but excited, their whole demeanor expressing eager anticipation of the daring venture.

SCOTT:
I got it from a native, Cap'n. They hate the Spanish worse than we do. Near as I could figure his lingo, the gold train leaves Venta Cruz at sundown . . . about seventy mules in all.

Carl whistles a long note that tells us he has translated seventy mules into gold and treasure.

THORPE:
The main caravan! . . . Listen, men, we'll spread out along the trail at intervals of ten yards. I'll stay at this point. Mr. Pitt, you across from me—then Mr. Scott next place down the line . . . Burke, I'm going to station you at the rear. Give a signal on your whistle when the last man and mule pass you. Then you all know what to do.

VOICES (ad lib):
Aye, Cap'n . . . That we do . . . We'll grab 'em . . . They won't get away . . . Etc.

THORPE:
Mr. Scott, how far is Venta Cruz from here?

SCOTT:
About twenty miles, Cap'n. It'll take a mule train most of the night.

THORPE:

Then we'll have time for some sleep after we lay out the ambush. Better pick out your "nests" before dark.

There is a noticeable hesitancy on the part of the company as they glance uneasily toward the jungle wall.

BEN:

It's dark enough now, Cap'n. Blimy, if it ain't creepy in there.

THORPE:

You can wait out on the trail until you hear the mule bells. (With Carl at his side he advances to the nearest edge of the tangled growth.)

SCOTT:

Come on, men—you heard what the Cap'n said.

Camera pans with Scott and the rest of the group as they file slowly down the trail, talking among themselves, walking away from Thorpe in the direction right to left.

BOGGS:

It's too thick. You can't see wot's in it.

BURKE:

Snakes and crocodiles, I'll wager.

Camera leaves the men and pans very slowly along the edge of the jungle. It looks dense and hot and still. The vegetation is unnaturally large. Great strong vines twine and twist around the trees.

BEN'S VOICE (over scene):

They say there's plants with arms like that'll strangle a man if he ain't careful . . .

SCOTT'S VOICE (over scene):

Lay off that talk, Ben, or you'll be seein' ghosts before you're seein' Spaniards.

The other men laugh, but the laughter is forced and nervous.

112.　MED. SHOT　THORPE AND CARL　EDGE OF JUNGLE
Thorpe is tearing apart some matted vines with his hands as Carl hacks away with his knife. Over scene is the buzzing of mosquitoes.

CARL:
> Funny about sailors. They don't mind a fight, but they like to see what they're fightin' . . . Now take a mosquito, for instance . . . Ouch! (He slaps his neck viciously, then begins to thresh his arms wildly.) Ouch! There's a whole nest of them!

Thorpe laughs at Carl's antics. Finally he shakes them off, comes back to the edge of the trail, and follows Thorpe cautiously.

THORPE:
> What were you saying about a mosquito?

CARL:
> Nothing. The beasts've got ears.

THORPE:
> Look, we're far enough in from the trail.

Through the opening they have made in the wall of vine and brush they peer into the jungle. The camera pans over the matted jungle floor to a swampy morass. There are strange, lush plants and vine-draped trees. The camera comes to rest on a single flower, exotic and shapely. The camera pulls closer to it, and we see it is of the orchid family, its delicate petals opened wide.

DISSOLVE TO:

113.　FULL SHOT　THE MARKETPLACE　LATE AFTERNOON
at Venta Cruz. The long treasure train is just starting out. Lieutenant Ortega rides on a horse at its head. The heavily laden mules are lined up in rows waiting their

turn to join the train. The natives lead them out one by one. To every five or six mules goes one native to keep them in order—and one Spanish guard, carrying a musket. (All are on foot.) The necks of the mules move up and down in a slow rhythm, ringing the deep-toned bells rhythmically. The caravan travels from left to right.

DISSOLVE TO:

114. MED. SHOT   SECTION OF JUNGLE TRACK
where we saw Thorpe and his men the afternoon before. It is about seven in the morning, but the sun doesn't yet reach the track directly; it comes through the jungle in slanting shafts of light at intervals, like sun through cathedral windows. There is a deathly hush on the place, broken only by the occasional, startling cry of a bird in the jungle.

Thorpe, Scott, and Carl are standing near together on the track looking somewhat anxious, listening. Thorpe glances up at the sky overhead at the slant of the sun's rays through the trees.

The camera pans along the track in the direction of Venta Cruz (from right to left) about twenty yards, where another sailor of the crew is waiting, sitting on his haunches, listening intently.

The camera pans along (from right to left) on the track to show more of Thorpe's men, all about twelve yards apart, all silently waiting and listening for the sound of the mules' bells.

(NOTE: This shall not be done in one continuous pan shot as it would take too much time to cover this. There should be various cuts of Thorpe's men, the camera traveling from right to left and just panning on the man and off him again, repeating this action with several of the characters. By cutting it together we will get the effect of a continuous pan shot.)

115. PAN SHOT   BURKE AND BOGGS
at the rear of the spread-out ambush. They look off to

the left. Like the others they are listening. On their faces comes the look of hearing something, then of doubting it, then straining to tell if it's imaginary or actual. Very, very faintly we hear the distant mule bells. Burke goes to the side of the track, parts the thick foliage, steps in, and disappears from view.

116.   EIGHT QUICK SHOTS
of one man after another hearing the bells, taking to his hiding place in the jungle on either side of the track; of Thorpe, Carl, Scott as they too hear them. Thorpe nods; they seek their jungle "nests"—Thorpe and Scott on one side of the track, Carl directly opposite.

CUT TO:

117.   BURKE AND BOGGS
crouched in their hiding place. The bells are quite loud by now. They are watching the track through the leaves, looking to the left.

118.   MED. SHOT   THE TRACK
Burke's angle, through the leaves. The legs of a horse pass by, the legs of a mule, another mule, the bare legs of a native, more mules, the wrapped legs of a Spanish soldier, more mules (traveling from left to right).

119.   OMITTED

120.   MED. SHOT   ORTEGA
riding slowly along. His face is still impassive, but his eyes dart from side to side of the jungle ahead of him, as if expecting something (traveling from left to right).

120A.   The camera has now taken the place of Ortega and travels forward on the trail (the jungle as if seen by Ortega). Nothing can be seen on the trail, and on either side the jungle is dark and dense, the leaves motionless.

121.   MED. CLOSE SHOT   THORPE AND SCOTT
in the jungle, waiting tensely (looking off to the left) as
the bells grow louder.

122.   LONG SHOT   JUNGLE TRACK
from above, showing a long section of the caravan,
wending its slow, rhythmic way between the walls of
the jungle (the caravan traveling from left to right).

123.   CLOSE SHOT   BURKE
crouched as before. He now has the whistle between his
lips, ready to blow, watching for the end of the mule
train.

123A.   EXTRA CUT   BURKE
watching. The last of the caravan just passes him. He
lets it pass another ten feet. He then blows his whistle.

124.   TWO-SHOT   THORPE AND SCOTT
The front of the caravan is almost up to them (as can be
judged by the sound of the bells. The horses' hooves are
now audible—the mules' hooves—the squeaking of the
panniers). Thorpe looks terribly anxious, fearing he has
not spread out his ambush enough. Suddenly there is
heard a shrill blast of a whistle, and both men spring out
onto the track.

125.   MED. SHOT   FRONT OF CARAVAN
Ortega in the lead, followed by mules, natives, and soldiers, moving single file along the jungle trail and toward the camera, as Thorpe and Carl spring out from
opposite sides. Ortega's horse rears when Carl grabs his
bridle. Thorpe's pistol covers the Spanish officer while
Scott pinions the arms of one of the escort soldiers a few
paces back.

THORPE:
Dismount, Lieutenant . . . (Ortega, showing no

surprise, swings down from the saddle.) Take his weapons, Mr. Pitt.

CARL:

Aye, Cap'n.

He advances on the officer. The camera pans down the line of the halted caravan to show what is apparently a perfectly executed surprise attack. At two different points we see English seamen with drawn cutlasses take prisoners without meeting any resistance from the seemingly dazed Spaniards or the indifferent natives. There is no fighting or confusion as the treasure train passes into English hands. The chief resistance comes from some of the mules that take the occasion to lie down under their heavy burdens, to the bewilderment of their new masters.

126.   MED. SHOT   FRONT OF CARAVAN   ORTEGA, THORPE, SCOTT, CARL

SCOTT (grins):

Looks like it's come pretty easy, Cap'n.

THORPE (with some concern):

Yes—almost too easy! Go down the line, Mr. Scott. See if everything's in our hands and ready to move.

Scott turns and goes off.

ORTEGA (protesting, but without much fervor):

This is an outrage! It will be reported to His Majesty, King Philip.

THORPE (ironically):

The news may be somewhat delayed in reaching His Majesty. I'll have to ask you to remain my prisoner.

ORTEGA (with excessive dignity):

Under protest, Captain Thorpe.

Thorpe is half turned away. Now he wheels around to look at Ortega more closely.

THORPE:
    So you know my name . . .

ORTEGA (covering his slip as best he can):
    Er—uh, yes, señor. Everyone in Spain knows your name . . . and respects it.

THORPE (still studying the Spaniard):
    I'm flattered, Lieutenant. (Significantly.) I shall have to warn you against any false move. My men would be forced to shoot you. (Ortega nods, mounts his horse.) Incidentally, if we should happen to pass anyone on the trail, this is *your* caravan and we're part of your escort, do you understand?

Ortega bows coldly; Thorpe and Carl fall in close behind him, Carl with a musket, Thorpe with a watchful hand at his pistol belt.

THORPE (calls back to the waiting line):
    We're ready to start. Pass the word, back there.

The procession moves slowly in the same direction (left to right). Camera remains fixed and we see six or seven mules pass, attended by a native, then two Spanish soldiers closely supervised by an armed Englishman directly in back of them.

127.   MED. SHOT   REAR OF CARAVAN
With might and main Boggs is trying to drag the last mule to his feet. This one happens to be an obstinate animal, unused to the methods of his new driver. Scott comes rushing up, laughs uproariously at the sight of Boggs wrestling with a mule while the native driver stands indifferently by.

BOGGS (ruffled):
    If you think it's so funny, try it yourself. The bloomin' beast must think it's *his* gold we're takin'.

Scott speaks a few words in native dialect to the Indian
driver, who, without changing his expression, walks
over to the mule and gently lifts his head. Immediately
the animal gets to his feet and starts obediently after the
procession. Boggs scratches his head with an "I'll-be-
damned" expression on his face.[23]

DISSOLVE TO:

127A. OMITTED

128. MED. SHOT   CLEARING NEAR JUNGLE
A detachment of cavalrymen ride into the clearing,
dismount, and leave the horses under the guidance of a
few soldiers. The balance of the men make their way
into the jungle (they enter the jungle in the direction
from right to left), camera panning with them for a few
feet as they go into the denseness of the jungle.

CUT TO:

128A. LONG SHOT   THORPE AND CARAVAN
walking (from left to right) through the jungle.

CUT TO:

128B. THE CAVALRY DETACHMENT
now on foot making their way on the jungle trail (in the
direction from right to left).

CUT TO:

128C. THORPE AND CARAVAN
making their way through the jungle (from left to right).

CUT TO:

128D. PRIMITIVE BRIDGE   IN JUNGLE
The cavalrymen, on foot, come near bridge, stop, get off
trail, and hide near bridge.
   (NOTE: Some of the cavalrymen will have laid explosives under the bridge, but I believe it wise not to show
this and have it come as a surprise when the bridge will
be blown up later.)

CUT TO:

128E. THORPE AND CARAVAN
coming along the trail in direction from left to right, and as the rear end of the caravan passes camera, the camera pans further to the left where we see that another pass joins the main trail on which Thorpe had been traveling. On this side pass we see another detachment of Spaniards on foot approaching the main trail slowly.

The camera stops on them and as they approach the main trail they jump off the trail and take their positions in the bushes, etc., of the jungle.

The camera keeps on panning to the right and we see the rear end of Thorpe's caravan just disappearing in the distance. The camera holds this a few seconds, and then the Spaniards who have been hiding on the right and left sides of the trail slowly start following in the direction Thorpe's caravan has disappeared.

128F–G. OMITTED

128H. PRIMITIVE BRIDGE IN JUNGLE
Camera over the back of Spaniards in ambush. In the distance we see Thorpe's caravan approaching. As they come closer and closer the Spanish officer gives the signal, and as Thorpe's men just are approaching the bridge it is blown to pieces. Thorpe's caravan comes to a sudden stop, the mules shy, and there is a salvo of guns from the Spaniards who are still hiding in ambush.

Thorpe and his men start shooting. (Thorpe's men are shooting from left to right. The Spaniards on this side of the blown-up bridge are shooting from right to left.)

Carl gives a shout, lifts his musket as he realizes the trap. Thorpe springs forward and with the flat side of his sword strikes Ortega's horse, plunging him head-on into the water (where bridge had been).

CUT TO:

128I. CLOSE SHOT CARL
aiming and shooting.

CUT TO:

128J. OTHER SIDE OF BRIDGE

as Spaniard is brought down by Carl's shot.

CUT BACK TO:

128K. THORPE AND CARL

THORPE (shouts; without turning his head from the attacking force):
    Back up . . . keep behind the mules.

CARL:
    Aye, Cap'n. It's a trap and no mistake!

But he is too busy to finish the sentence and several Spanish muskets answer his fire. Camera trucks with the pair as they retreat, attempting to turn the mules sideways to obstruct the path of the Spaniards who are now following on foot, shooting pistols as they come. Thorpe raises his pistol and picks off the closest one while ducking behind the frightened, disorganized mules, as pistols and muskets are emptied at him. As the camera trucks back along the line, we now pick up one of the captured Spanish escort soldiers reaching for a dagger concealed under a mule pannier. With his attention focused on the front, Thorpe is unconsciously backing right into the waiting Spaniard who stands poised with his knife. His arm raises to plunge it into Thorpe's back, when Eli, advancing from behind, sees the danger, hurdles an obstructing mule, and tackles the Spaniard before the dagger descends on Thorpe. Eli's knife flashes and the Spaniard lies still.

THORPE (over his shoulder):
    Good work, Eli . . .

ELI (springing to Thorpe's side):
    The beggars were ready for us, Cap'n.

THORPE:
    Why don't the others come up?

ELI:

Trouble in the rear, maybe . . .

Carl is hard pressed at this juncture by three cavalrymen who are converging on him with swords. He
slashes away with the cutlass. One goes down. The
other two nearly have him when Thorpe falls on them
from the side, while Eli fends off others attempting to
close in on Thorpe.

CUT TO:

129.   MED. SHOT   REAR OF THE CARAVAN
where the other Spanish force has simultaneously attacked. Scott, Burke, and a half dozen of the crew are
fighting desperately to stem the assault. But superior
numbers are pressing them back (left to right).

CUT TO:

129A.   MED. SHOT   FRONT END OF CARAVAN
Thorpe and his men are slowly pressed back (in the
direction from right to left) by the advancing Spaniards.

CUT TO:

129B.   OMITTED

130.   QUICK SHOTS
A. Of Winters shot at close range by a charging
Spaniard. He drops under the surging mules.
B. Of Monty Preston stabbed in the back by a Spanish
convoy soldier. To hold him up he grasps a pannier but
goes down with the mule and pannier on top of him.
C. Omitted.
D. Of Scott, who is putting up a magnificent fight and
enjoying it. He slugs, slashes, and kicks as four
Spaniards surround him. Two go down under his
windmill defense, but the third knocks him on the head
with the butt of his musket. For a moment Scott
disappears, then pops up unexpectedly on the other
side of a prancing mule. With his fist he knocks down
the man that struck him.

E. Of Arnold Cross, who is locked with a Spaniard just inside the jungle wall. In the violence of their struggle, they tear through the tangled vines and roll into a swampy morass. With a stranglehold around each other's necks, they sink together into the murky water.

CUT AGAIN TO:

131. OMITTED

131A. OMITTED

131B. LONG SHOT
where Thorpe (on right side of frame) and Eli and men from rear of caravan (on left side of frame) are slowly, foot by foot, being pressed together by the onrushing Spanish forces which come from the right as well as from the left.

Thorpe, Carl, and Eli are now united, back to back, with the retreating survivors of the rear guard of the company. The group, now reduced to ten battered and wounded men, are sandwiched in between the two Spanish forces, both vastly superior in numbers. The Spanish officers shout encouraging commands to their men as they close in to finish off the defenders. The English derive some protection from the milling mules and clumsy panniers that hamper the Spanish in the confined space of the trail.[24]

132. MED. CLOSE SHOT   THORPE AND HIS MEN
Bloody, staggering, but still resisting. Thorpe glances about him, sees that there is no chance to cut their way through either front or rear.

THORPE (shouts):
The jungle[25] . . . all of you . . . quick! Cut your way through!

With one thrust he slashes an opening in the jungle wall at the nearest point while Carl and Eli fend off the nearest attackers. The three then suddenly turn and leap into the dense growth. The camera pans a short distance down the trail and we see the English break their way through the tangled wall at various points. One man is stuck in the meshed vines, and a Spaniard's sword pierces him through the middle, his body hanging limply in the brush. Several Spaniards rush to follow the defeated crew into the jungle, but an officer, riding up on his horse, shouts to them.

SPANISH OFFICER:
Back to your command! Out of the jungle, you fools! No one can live in there! Do you hear? Back to your command!

The few soldiers who have dared to venture off the trail return to the track, which is strewn with the dead and wounded.

DISSOLVE TO:

133. MED. LONG SHOT   IN THE JUNGLE
Thorpe, Tom, Carl, Tuttle, Burke, and Eli. They are trying to run, but the growth is so thick and tangled that they are constantly held up, tripped, impeded. With the exception of Tuttle, who is following Thorpe's path, with his arm held across his chest, each man is picking his own way—Carl and Eli hacking wildly at the vines with their cutlasses, Burke with a smaller knife. Presently Thorpe stops to listen on the ground—the others halt. The jungle is gloomy and still.

THORPE:
No one's following. We can rest. (All the men sink to the ground exhausted. Thorpe turns to Tuttle and starts very gently to lift away the arm from his chest.) Let me see your arm, William . . .

TUTTLE (obviously in great pain, drawing back his arm): It's in my chest, Captain . . . a piece of musket lead.

THORPE (gently):
We'll take it out when we get to the ship.

TUTTLE (smiles, but in the way he smiles we know he will never get back to the ship):
Yes, Captain.

CARL (abruptly, to change the subject):
What I can't figger is how the Spaniards knew we were here.

THORPE (grimly):
Some day we'll find out . . . Well, we'd better move on.

He helps Tuttle to his feet. The others get up. They look pretty bad. Carl has a knife cut on his forehead; Scott is limping. All are dripping with perspiration, stifling in the deadly heat of the jungle.

SCOTT:
Wonder if the others got through, Cap'n?

THORPE (briefly):
They'll head for the ship if they did.

The men are struggling again to make some progress— not in haste to elude pursuers this time, but in haste to be out of the choking jungle. The sudden, shrill cry of a bird startles them for a moment.

DISSOLVE TO:

134–37. OMITTED

138. CLOSE SHOT   BEN   IN ANOTHER PART OF THE JUNGLE
sitting on some big tangled roots, rocking back and forth with his head in his hands, a trickle of blood running out through his fingers, his eyes staring and bloodshot.

BEN (delirious; talking as if he saw men around him):
It's too hot . . . it's too bloody hot . . . Let's get out of here, you fool . . . You sneakin' Spaniards—you

low, stinkin' swine . . . (Under the whip of his fury, he rises uncertainly to his feet and staggers a few yards, then looks around dazed. Every direction appears the same—an impenetrable green maze.) How do you get out of here? (He lurches, falls, and lies rolling on his back, holding his head.) Get away . . . get out of my way . . . I'm going to the ship, you fools . . . It's too bloody hot . . . too hot . . . (Rolls over on his face.)

DISSOLVE TO:

139.   THORPE'S GROUP
Now in a very thickly matted part of the jungle. Thorpe is in the lead, cutting a path, the others in single file behind him with Carl in the rear carrying Tuttle, who now appears to be unconscious. All are so weak that they stumble and grab at the trees and vines for support. Presently Thorpe stops, turns around. He is too exhausted to speak with emotion.

THORPE:
Water—just ahead—through the trees.

Camera pans over Scott, Eli, Burke, Carl. In the eyes of all we read the incredulity of men who had given up hope of life.

140.   MED. SHOT   THE EDGE OF THE JUNGLE
at the cove where they left their small boats. The men emerge from the jungle and make for the water as if they were on fire. They fall in it, submerge their heads, too weak to do anything but lie down like animals in the shallow water. Thorpe goes to Carl, who is kneeling, supporting Tuttle.

141.   MED. CLOSE SHOT   THORPE, CARL, TUTTLE
As Thorpe puts water on the old man's face and head, Tuttle's eyes open. He looks around him, sees the water.

TUTTLE (faint smile):
    You did it, Cap'n . . .

Thorpe looks out seaward to where the *Albatross* lies, and we know that he never expected to see his ship again, and that in spite of his sick heart, he is glad to see her.

THORPE:
    Yes, we did it.

142.   LONG SHOT   THE ALBATROSS
    bobbing gently on the waves, the flags fluttering gaily at her masts.[26]

DISSOLVE TO:

143.   MED. SHOT   THE SIX SURVIVORS (PROCESS) NEAR SUNDOWN
    in one of the small pinnaces, rowing out to the *Albatross*. (We avoid showing the small boat and the *Albatross* in the same shot until the pinnace is directly alongside the ship.) Thorpe and Carl do the rowing. Tuttle is lying against some rope in the bow. All the men are thinking of their lost companions, of what this trip back to the *Albatross* was to have meant, of the men waiting there for them with high hopes.

SCOTT (looking off toward the ship):
    It's hard news to carry back . . .

ELI (pause):
    They'll be wonderin' now why just the one boat's comin'.

BURKE (pause):
    Some of them might get through yet . . . (fearfully, nursing a slender hope) might they, Cap'n?

THORPE (after a pause):
    It's a miracle any of us are here, Burke.

There is a long silence now as the oars dip rhythmically in the water.

ELI (squinting off through his cupped fingers):
I don't see the lookout . . .

SCOTT (bitterly):
They didn't expect us so soon.

144. FULL SHOT   THE ALBATROSS
closer now but with none of the crew left to guard her in sight. The ship appears dark in contrast to the lighter background of the sunset sky.

145. MED. CLOSE SHOT   THE PINNACE

BURKE (his eyes glued on the *Albatross*):
Funny they ain't posted a lookout.

SCOTT:
May be one behind the charthouse. We couldn't see him from here.

ELI:
'Ope they ain't got in the ale closet. I could do with a mug if the chaps ain't drunk it all up.

BURKE (wearily):
All I want is to sleep for a thousand years.

ELI (pointing at Tuttle):
'Ere's one wot beat you to it. (His face screws up as he looks closer at the sleeping man.) Cap'n! (Thorpe and Carl stop rowing, turn around while the pinnace drifts on. Eli is gently shaking Tuttle. No response from Tuttle. Eli turns slowly, faces the others, speaks softly, brokenly.) 'E oin't never goin' to wake up.

THORPE (after a silence, he speaks gently):
He got back to the sea.

Eli covers the dead man with a piece of canvas that he finds at the bottom of the pinnace as Thorpe and Carl continue to row. For a few moments, there is only the sound of the oars.

CARL (over his shoulder):
Sight anyone on the boat yet?

BURKE:
Not a bloomin' soul.

THORPE:
Call to them, Scott. We'll need their help at the ladder.

SCOTT (calls loudly):
Ahoy there! . . . Ahoy, mates! Give us a hand!

146.   MED. LONG SHOT
The *Albatross* much closer now, but still shrouded in silence.

SCOTT (over scene; calls with growing indignation):
You lubbers, show your faces . . . ! It's the Cap'n . . . Do you hear me? IT'S THE CAP'N!

147.   MED. SHOT   THE PINNACE

THORPE:
Never mind.

ELI (scratching his head):
What are the blasted fools 'idin' for!

BURKE:
I don't like it. Somethin's wrong.

CARL (stops rowing):
Burke, lay off that talk or I'll—

THORPE:
Easy now, men; we're almost there.

SCOTT:
Maybe the lads swam ashore.

ELI:
Not a chance. Too many sharks.

Suddenly the dark hull of the *Albatross* looms alongside their boat. Scott catches hold of the rope ladder as Thorpe and Carl put down the oars.

THORPE:
> Burke, you stay here. The rest of you come with me.

AD LIB:
> Aye, Cap'n . . . All right, Cap'n . . . Etc.

Thorpe begins to climb up the ladder with Carl and the others close behind him.

148. MED. SHOT MAIN DECK OF THE ALBATROSS
as Thorpe and Carl and others come over the rail. There is an unnatural silence over the ship. The masts and rigging with the setting sun behind them throw spectral shadows across the silent deck. Thorpe and Carl look toward the deserted foc's'le and exchange mystified glances. They take a few wary steps toward the quarter-deck when the starboard door suddenly opens and a trim Spanish officer steps out. He stands regarding the astonished survivors with a smile both amused and sinister. The Spanish officer is none other than Captain López, whose ship was previously sunk by the *Albatross*.

LÓPEZ:
> Welcome, Captain Thorpe. (Thorpe's hand slips down to the hilt of his sword, and Carl reaches for his dagger—the only weapons the survivors have left.) I should not advise you to resist.

As he speaks the camera pans to doors, windows, hatchways—all with leveled muskets partly concealed in the darkness.

LÓPEZ'S VOICE (over scene):
> There are sixteen muskets pointed at you—all expert marksmen, I assure you. Besides, it's my turn

to entertain *you*. I regret it has to be on your ship
. . . (Grim.) But you will understand the necessity.

149.　MED. SHOT   LÓPEZ, THORPE, AND SURVIVORS
Thorpe's hand tightens on the sword hilt as his glance
appraises the chances for a desperate break. Carl and
the others wait for Thorpe's signal.

LÓPEZ:
If you draw that sword, Captain, we shall *not* have
the pleasure of taking you and your men back to
Spain . . . *alive*.

Obviously, there is no chance of escape. Thorpe's hand
relaxes, drops hopelessly to his side. He bows slightly,
speaks with quiet dignity.

THORPE:
Your prisoners, Captain López.
　　　　　　　　　　　　　　　　　　FADE OUT

FADE IN
150.　MED. SHOT   INQUISITION TRIBUNAL
a tomblike room, dimly lit by candles, with two cowled
figures visible at a long table attended by armed guards
on either side. Facing the table about ten feet away, their
hands tied behind their backs, are the survivors of the
Albatross: Thorpe slightly in front, Carl, Scott, Eli, and
Burke. The Englishmen listen with cool defiance to the
words of the chief inquisitor. (It is suggested that the
word "inquisitor" and related words with direct reli-
gious connotation be omitted from dialogue so that the
nature of the tribunal will only be visually inferred. Also
that historical validity be preserved by prefacing
Thorpe's crimes with the charge of sorcery—an
ecclesiastical offense and one widely attributed to Drake
by the Spanish.)[27]

INQUISITOR (grim, droning voice):
. . . Item thirty-seven: You did by sorcery and
other heretical practices contrive to enter secretly by

night the Spanish city of Cartagena, and did capture the garrison and force the governor thereof to pay a ransom in the amount of thirty thousand ducats . . . Item thirty-eight: You did also attack His Majesty's galleass, *Madre Dolores*, at Valparaiso and did seize gold in the amount of eight thousand pounds, thirteen chests of coined silver, and one thousand seven hundred seventy jars of wine . . . Item thirty-nine: You did also loot and sink the galleass *Santa Eulalia del Monte* in the English Channel, profaning His Majesty in the person of his ambassador . . . In summary of these offenses our records show you did plunder seven cities in the Empire of Spain and did destroy forty-seven of His Majesty's vessels . . . Captain Thorpe, do you confess to the truth of these charges?

THORPE:
Your records do us an injustice, señor . . .

The inquisitor looks from his paper, waits for Thorpe to proceed.

THORPE (with grim irony):
They should read *nine* cities and *fifty-four* ships.

INQUISITOR (impassively to his fellow inquisitor, who is making notes on the proceeding):
You will amend the charges in accordance with the defendant's statement and place his confession on record. (Turning back to the prisoners.) It is adjudged you will be handed over to the military authorities, under whose direction you will be chained to the oars of a galley in servitude for the rest of your natural lives . . .[28]

Voice fading as we

DISSOLVE TO:

151. CLOSE SHOT   CHAIN STAPLE IN GALLEY
A heavy iron is being driven deep into the hardwood
wall by blows from a sledgehammer. From the staple a
long chain runs through the rings on all the leg cuffs of
the men on that oar. When the staple is embedded
down to its head, camera pans up to reveal Eli on the
inside wall of the ship's hold, then along the bench to
another slave (a stranger), and finally to Thorpe on the
end of the rowers' bench next to the runway.

152. MED. LONG SHOT   THE HOLD OF THE GALLEY
The rowers sit deep in the hold, so that their view is cut
off behind the walls of the galley. The wide center runway is used for a freight deck except at the sides, where
the slave master stands with his whip. Carl is seated in
the row directly in front of Thorpe, while Tom and
Burke are seated on a third bench. All the men are
stripped of their clothes except for breechclouts. The
same type of gavel and wooden block arrangement is
used for beating out the rowing time. The captain of the
galley appears, coming down the stairway from the
quarterdeck, and stands at the stern end of the runway.
He looks over the chained slaves with satisfaction, his
eyes finally resting on Thorpe, who sits facing him.

MENDOZA:
> Captain Thorpe . . . or perhaps we can dispense
> with the "captain" under the circumstances. (He
> smiles. Thorpe sits very still, waiting.) It is not often
> that we have the pleasure of entertaining such a
> famous pirate in our galley. (With cruel meaning.) I
> hope that you find our hospitality all that you an-
> ticipated.

THORPE (with biting scorn):
> No doubt we shall, señor. Your people have a gift
> for hospitality when their guests are in chains.

Mendoza's face clouds. The slave master's whip curls

around Thorpe's back. The English sailors strain on
their chains, but Thorpe gives no sign of anger or pain.

MENDOZA (to the slave master):
> We are putting out of port. You will start the oars at
> twelve beats.

SLAVE MASTER:
> Yes, Captain. (Mendoza turns and ascends the
> stairway.) Oars in the water! Now pull, you English
> mongrels . . . one, two, three . . . one, two, three
> . . .

The timekeeper takes up the count on the block. The
men lean on their oars, pull them back in unison, bend
forward again as we

DISSOLVE TO:

153.   CLOSE SHOT   MARIA
singing to the accompaniment of a lute. The words are
in English. Camera pulls back to show Maria in the
queen's chamber, surrounded by the maids of honor,
with Elizabeth listening intently.[29] The song comes to an
end and the girls applaud Maria, who looks toward the
queen to know her pleasure.

ELIZABETH:
> But are all Spanish songs so sad, my child?

MARIA:
> Only those that speak of love, Your Grace.

ELIZABETH (shrewdly):
> You speak of it eloquently, my dear. (More to her-
> self than to the others.) I dare say each of us must
> choose between loving a man or ruling him. I prefer
> to rule. (As Maria turns her head slightly the queen
> speaks very gently.) I don't quarrel with your
> choice, Maria. You have your song and I have my
> scepter . . . But now sing us one that is gay.

Before Maria can begin an usher appears before the queen and bows to her.

USHER:

>Your pardon, Majesty . . . His Excellency, Don Alvarez, begs an immediate audience.

ELIZABETH (angrily):

>Then let him choose a more fitting time. (The usher bows, starts to turn away when the queen thinks better of her words.) Wait . . . I shall grant him an interview. But warn him to be brief. (The usher bows, walks toward the door.) You see, Maria, the scepter also carries its penalties.

154.   MED. SHOT   DOOR OF CHAMBER

as the usher opens it to Don Alvarez, who walks toward the queen.

155.   TWO-SHOT   ELIZABETH AND ALVAREZ

Alvarez bows to the queen.

ELIZABETH:

>Well, is your business so urgent, Don Alvarez, that it must intrude upon my few moments of diversion?

ALVAREZ:

>Your Grace, I have just had a communication from Spain that I feel sure will command your interest . . . It concerns the privateer, Francis Thorpe.

ELIZABETH (concealing her eagerness):

>Yes? What about him?

Camera pans to the maids of honor, all attending closely, and holds on Maria, who waits in breathless suspense.

ALVAREZ (over scene):

>While attempting a raid on the Panama treasure

train, he was captured by Spanish troops and is now a condemned prisoner on one of His Majesty's galleys.

Maria sinks to the floor in a faint.

MAIDS OF HONOR (ad lib):
Maria! She is ill! She's fainted!

Camera draws back to show Elizabeth standing anxiously. Alvarez, with a puzzled and concerned expression, walks toward his niece, who quickly recovers from the shock. Assisted by two maids of honor, she rises somewhat shakily to her feet.

ALVAREZ:
Maria, my child . . .

MARIA:
It is nothing, Uncle . . . (Turns to the queen.) Your pardon, Majesty, for . . .

ELIZABETH:
Say no more, my dear. I quite understand. (To the other maids.) You will take Maria to her rooms and stay with her as long as she needs you.

MARIA:
My thanks, Your Grace. (She bows. With the other girls anxiously following her, she turns to go out.)

156.   MED. SHOT   THE QUEEN AND ALVAREZ

ELIZABETH (craftily):
Don Alvarez, it appears your news concerns your niece more than it does me.

ALVAREZ:
Your Majesty, I would have spared her had I known.

ELIZABETH:
Very well; your arrow hit the wrong mark . . . As

for myself, I regret Captain Thorpe's fate because he is a brave man. But he is a privateer and privateers take their own risks.

ALVAREZ:
Your Grace, I must speak bluntly. My sovereign is not convinced that Captain Thorpe risked so much merely for his own gain.

ELIZABETH:
No? Then perhaps you will suggest a more likely motive.

ALVAREZ:
Your Grace will recall that she released Thorpe after his attack upon my ship, and that, on the heels of this offense, she allowed the *Albatross* to sail, presumably to trade in Egypt.

ELIZABETH:
Well, am I to be held accountable for Captain Thorpe's change of mind?

ALVAREZ (respectfully, but firmly):
Your Majesty, Thorpe never intended any project but the one he undertook . . . although by now he might wish he had.

ELIZABETH (irritably):
Don Alvarez, you weary me with your implications. Come to the point.

ALVAREZ:
I regret that the point is not an agreeable one. From these circumstances I mentioned, my sovereign is forced to infer that Captain Thorpe had the approval of Your Majesty in an overt act of war against the Empire of Spain.

ELIZABETH (flaring up):
Don Alvarez! Do you question my word!

ALVAREZ (holding his ground):
Unfortunately, Your Majesty, my government cannot reconcile your words with the acts of your subjects.

ELIZABETH (snaps):
Then let Philip infer what he pleases.

ALVAREZ:
In that case I am instructed to serve official notice upon Your Majesty . . . that the honor of Spain requires that you will immediately disband and imprison the Sea Hawks or face the consequences of an open conflict between our two nations.

ELIZABETH (rises in a dangerous temper):
What are you saying? Do you dare come to me with threats? Out of my court! Do you hear? Before I order your arrest . . .

Alvarez bows stiffly, turns on his heel, and walks off. In his cool dignity we sense the advantage of his position over the queen, who is pacing the floor, beside herself with rage. The usher comes forward. Perceiving Elizabeth's mood, he approaches with some hesitancy. She turns to him.

ELIZABETH:
Go to Lord Wolfingham. Tell him to summon my council at once . . . No, wait. (Indicating Philip's portrait on the wall.) First remove that man's picture from my sight. (The attendant hesitates, looks from the picture to the queen, who stamps her foot.) Hurry! Do as I say! (He turns helplessly toward the picture as Elizabeth continues to pace the room.) Presumptuous fool! Telling me what I must do . . . Has Philip gone mad? Does he imagine he can dictate to the Queen of England!

DISSOLVE TO:

157. MED. SHOT COUNCIL ROOM
Elizabeth at the head of the council table. On her right
Lord Wolfingham, on her left Sir John Burleson. Behind
them are seated Lords Darnell, Hormiston, and
Hughes, members of the queen's privy council. We
realize immediately that Elizabeth's passionate temper
has given way to her shrewd, businesslike judgment,
always manifest when England's vital interests are at
stake. Burleson is in the midst of pleading the cause of
the Sea Hawks.

BURLESON:
. . . But, Your Grace, this demand is preposterous. These men are loyal and devoted. In what way
have they offended but in serving their country?
. . . Spain seeks to strip you of your one defense
on the seas.

WOLFINGHAM:
Sir John, we need defense only if we are attacked.
To disregard Philip's warning is to invite an im-
mediate war.

BURLESON:
While to heed it is to throw ourselves at his mercy.

WOLFINGHAM:
And what of that? He has too many concerns else-
where to bother about us . . .

BURLESON:
My lord, I feel convinced that Philip's thirst for
power can only be quenched in the English Channel.

WOLFINGHAM (cynically):
Even if that were true, are my lord admiral and his
privateers prepared to stop him?

BURLESON (simply, but with depth of feeling):
We are ready to try, my lord . . . to the last ship
and to the last man.

There is a silence around the table. Elizabeth flashes her admiral a look of grateful pride, but at the next instant she is again the calculating statesman, weighing her chances.

ELIZABETH:
Lord Darnell, we have not heard your opinion.

DARNELL:
Your Grace, I regret the sacrifice of the Sea Hawks quite as much as Sir John, but my judgment favors Lord Wolfingham's policy. By appeasing Philip we shall gain time.

HORMISTON (breaking in):
Time, Your Majesty, badly needed for defensive measures, to improve our chances against the Armada.

ELIZABETH (after a moment's pause):
My lords, I have considered your opinions earnestly. My own impulse, like Sir John's, is to defy Philip; but the safety of my subjects constrains me to caution. (In a flat voice, looking straight ahead of her.) Lord Wolfingham, you will prepare an order authorizing the arrest of all English privateers and the confiscation of their ships as they put into port.

Wolfingham conceals his satisfaction, rises, followed by the others, except Burleson. They bow to the queen and file out of the room. Burleson sits very still, his head lowered. When the others leave, the queen puts a compassionate hand on the old man's arm.

ELIZABETH (with deep feeling, in a rare moment of self-revelation):
My friend, there are times when a queen must think not of right or wrong, but only of the good of those she rules.

DISSOLVE TO:

158. MED. SHOT MARIA'S APARTMENT
Maria has thrown herself on a settle, is weeping as if her heart would break. Miss Latham is seated next to her, doing her best to comfort her.

MISS LATHAM:
My child, you mustn't despair.

MARIA (sobbing):
But the galley . . .

MISS LATHAM:
He's still alive, Maria.

MARIA (taking some hope):
Yes, he's still alive.

Alvarez comes in quietly. Maria turns away. Miss Latham rises, glares at Alvarez, and walks out of the room. Alvarez takes no notice of Miss Latham's look, walks to Maria, puts a sympathetic hand on her shoulder.

ALVAREZ:
I'm sorry, Maria.

MARIA:
If any harm comes to him, I'll never forgive you.

ALVAREZ:
My child, I only did what I had to do.

MARIA:
I'll never be happy as long as—

ALVAREZ:
Come, come—you're very young, Maria. Time will make you feel differently.

MARIA:
Uncle, if we went to Spain and plead with the king . . . (She stops as Alvarez shakes his head.) There's no chance?

ALVAREZ:

For any other man, perhaps—but not Captain Thorpe.

Maria breaks down and sobs again. As Alvarez tries ineffectually to comfort her we

DISSOLVE TO:

159.   MONTAGE

A. A montage to show the passage of days and weeks in the galley, an unbroken succession of horrors. The motif is the steady, relentless beat of the wooden mallet on the galley block, the sweep of the oars, foaming through the water, and the incessant lashing of the whip.

B. Shot embracing Thorpe and two other men at their oar, their skin burned, their faces drawn with suffering—bearded, unkempt—straining, tugging.

C. The fat Spanish timekeeper, drinking wine and eating meat as he pounds out the time.

D. Faces of the thirsty rowers watching him.

E. Full shot of straining backs of the slaves pulling. Their backs are scarred and dripping with perspiration.

F. Night shot of rowers.

G. The mallet pounding.

H. The whip lashing.

I. Oars beating out the stroke.

From letter "F" on, all the shots are played at night. Over the last few inserts we have heard a ship's bell and commands from the various officers yelling out orders which indicate a maneuver that they are pulling into a harbor. One of the final commands that comes over the last shots of the montage is to stop rowing. (These orders to be gotten from the expert who will be on the picture.)[30]

DISSOLVE TO:

160.   OMITTED

161.   OMITTED

162.   OMITTED

163.   TOP DECK   NIGHT
The officer boards the ship, walks over to the captain of
the galley, salutes.

SPANISH OFFICER (hands him papers):
Important dispatches.

Mendoza glances over them.

MENDOZA:
Very well. I'll see that they reach the *Madre de Dios*
before she sails from Cádiz.

The officer salutes and exits. Mendoza walks over to
where the four prisoners have been brought up under
guard.

GUARD OFFICER:
Captain, four prisoners assigned to your galley.

MENDOZA:
We'll put them to good use. Keep them in irons.
(He turns on his heel as the guards brutally push
them off scene.)

                                        DISSOLVE TO:

164.   MED. CLOSE SHOT   THORPE   DAY
on the galley, rowing regularly, listlessly. His face is
thinner, his beard heavy. Camera pulls back to show the
other two men on the oar. The slave next to Thorpe is
grotesquely gaunt and has practically no strength left to
row. Eli is sitting next. Camera moves back to include
the oar in front, where we see Carl and two strangers,
the oar in front of that where we see one stranger,
Burke, and Tom, all in much the same condition as
Thorpe, dazed, emaciated, rowing mechanically.

165.   FULL SHOT   THE WAIST OF THE GALLEY   DAY
showing all the slaves, the timekeeper beating out the
rhythm, the slave master sitting above them in the
stern, keeping an eye on all. As we watch he gets to his
feet, walks down the runway.

166.   MED. SHOT   AT THE OARS   DAY
where Thorpe and his men are rowing. We see that the
man next to Thorpe has stopped rowing, is sagged over
his oars. The slave master approaches with his whip.

SLAVE MASTER:
Get rowing, you . . . (He snaps his whip across the
man's bruised back.) Pull on that oar, do you hear!
(As he snaps the whip again, the man still not stirring.) I'm tired of your tricks . . .

The other men have all gone on rowing during this,
their glassy eyes straight ahead, no break in the rhythm
of their stroke. At this point Thorpe, as he leans forward
on his oar, turns his head and looks at the slave's face.
On the back stroke he turns to the slave master.

THORPE (no expression):
He's dead. (And he goes on rowing, without having broken the stroke.)

DISSOLVE TO:

167.   THE SAME SHOT
as previously only now there is the English spy that was
previously taken aboard with the other three prisoners,
sitting next to Thorpe. He looks very fit and fresh in
contrast to the others.

168.   CLOSE TWO-SHOT   THORPE AND ABBOTT   DAY
As they row Abbott looks at Thorpe, appears to be trying to place him, looks at him again, puzzled, and then
suddenly recognizes him. He almost cries out, controls
himself in time, and waits until they are both bending
over their oar, then whispers excitedly.

ABBOTT:

> Captain Thorpe! I didn't know you at first . . .
> (Thorpe turns his head toward the man but his face
> is quite blank. On the next forward stroke Abbott
> whispers to him again.) I was caught in Madrid
> . . . *Sir John sent me to Spain* . . . The Armada . . .
> (Another pause for the backward pull and the lift,
> then they go forward on the oar again; whispers
> fast.) Moving against England . . . soon. (For the
> first time some life appears in Thorpe's face. The
> dazed look leaves his eyes and we can see that he is
> taking in Abbott's words. On the next forward
> stroke, Abbott continues.) Sir John wanted proof
> . . . to convince the queen.

By this time Thorpe's eyes are alert, aroused from his
stupor by realization of the enormous threat to his beloved England. When they are bent forward again, he
addresses Abbott.

THORPE:

> The Sea Hawks—do they know?

ABBOTT (bitterly):

> They're all in prison—or hiding . . . by orders from
> Spain . . . The queen did it to avert war.

Thorpe looks profoundly shocked. His whole body has
taken on a new energy under the significance of Abbott's words.

THORPE (same procedure as they row):

> The Armada . . . Did you find proof?

ABBOTT:

> The papers are on this ship . . . taking them to the
> *Madre de Dios* in Cádiz . . . They had me before I
> could get them.

THORPE (grimly):

> They were informed. Same thing at Panama. (He
> rows for a moment in silence, his mind searching

for some desperate plan. Presently he speaks to Abbott.) Pass the word . . . when I stop rowing everyone stop . . . refuse to start . . . no matter what . . .

Abbott nods. On the next forward stroke, he turns to Eli and whispers. Just then a voice is heard calling from above, in the stern.

CAPTAIN'S VOICE (off scene):
Slave master!

169.   FULL SHOT   WAIST OF THE GALLEY   DAY

CAPTAIN'S VOICE (off scene):
Slave master! Up on deck!

The slave master rises, starts up the stairway to the quarterdeck.

SLAVE MASTER:
Coming, Captain!

170.   MED. SHOT   QUARTERDECK   CAPTAIN, SLAVE MASTER   DAY

SLAVE MASTER (arriving):
Yes, sir?

CAPTAIN (frowning, tapping a packet of papers in his hand):
We must reach Cádiz before the *Madre de Dios* sails— (Irritably.) Can't you raise the beat?

SLAVE MASTER:
They can't row above eighteen for long, Captain . . . What time does the *Madre de Dios* leave Cádiz?

CAPTAIN:
Before morning, that's all I know . . . And, I can't risk missing her . . . (Suddenly looking off over the side of the boat.) What's happened! We're slowing down.

The slave master looks startled too. We realize that the sound of the oars has stopped—the boat is barely moving.

171. ANGLE SHOT FROM ABOVE THE OARS   DAY
on one side of the galley. They are in the water but all perfectly still.

172. TWO-SHOT CAPTAIN AND SLAVE MASTER   DAY

CAPTAIN:
> The timekeeper is asleep . . . Quick—find out what's wrong . . .

The slave master leaps for the stairway leading down into the hold.

173. FULL SHOT WAIST OF GALLEY   DAY
Slave master comes rushing down the stairs. The timekeeper is still beating out the rhythm, but every slave sits motionless. The slave master grabs up his whip and charges down the runway.

SLAVE MASTER (in a bewildered rage):
> What are you sitting there for! Have you lost your senses! In the name of Satan I'll fix you, every one of you filthy dogs!

As there is still no movement on the part of the slaves, the slave master becomes wild in his fury. He steps down off the runway and begins to lash them at close range unmercifully.

174. MED. PAN SHOT SLAVE MASTER   DAY
moving beside the slaves.

SLAVE MASTER (hysterically):
> Pick up those oars! Before I kill every last one of you!

As the slave master passes close by, Carl sticks out his

foot and trips him just as the man in front pushes him backward. Carl grabs him up; the slaves get their hands on him, toss him around as he screams in panic.

SLAVE MASTER:
Help! Help! Hurry!

The Spaniard is jerked about, kicked, and viciously mauled by the insurgent slaves. Suddenly we hear the sound of running footsteps.

175.   CLOSE SHOT   SLAVE MASTER   DAY
over the men's heads. Thorpe's hand reaches out, closes around the hilt of the Spaniard's dagger, draws it from its scabbard. Camera pans down to show Thorpe thrusting the dagger under his bench.

176.   MED. LONG SHOT   WAIST OF GALLEY   DAY
near the scuffle, as Mendoza and two Spanish seamen arrive on the scene, running.

SPANIARDS AD LIB:
Here, let go, you! English dogs! Rebel, will you!

There is a bruising struggle as the slaves defend themselves as best they can. They swing their heavy chains at the charging Spaniards and bring two of them down. However, they are unable to follow up their advantage because of the leg-cuffs which hold them to their benches. Their captors finally get their hands on the slave master, who is badly beaten. They drag him up on the runway, where he lies moaning.

SEAMAN (picking up the slave master's whip, brandishes it over the slaves):
Shall I give it to 'em, Captain?

MENDOZA:
Not now. Stay with them and see they keep rowing. (Looking over at the slaves.) Thorpe, this is your work. When we make Cádiz, I'll see you hung!

Now pick up your oars and put your backs into it
. . . Timekeeper, keep the beat at twenty.

Mendoza turns, starts up the stairway, followed by a
seaman who is half-carrying the battered slave master.
As the timekeeper starts beating out the strokes and the
slaves begin their rhythm again we

CUT TO:

177.   THORPE
who looks down (camera pans down) to insert of dagger.

DISSOLVE TO:

178.   INSERT   ON BACK OF BOAT   NIGHT
reading:

MADRE DE DIOS[31]
CÁDIZ

Camera pans up to deck of boat, and we see sailors
throwing ropes over to the galley, which are then
grabbed by other sailors, and thereby they pull the two
boats close together. A gangplank is put across, and
Mendoza, with the papers he has received in the previous sequence, crosses over to the *Madre de Dios*. He is
greeted by an officer on the *Madre de Dios*.

OFFICER (saluting him):
Captain Ortiz has been expecting you.

MENDOZA:
Thank you.

He follows the officer into the interior of the boat. (NOTE:
It is observed that very few guards are in evidence on
either boat.)

DISSOLVE TO:

179.   OMITTED

180.   MED. LONG SHOT   HOLD OF THE GALLEY
as the lights are blown out. Moonlight strikes the galley.

On the benches the slaves are falling asleep in their chains. Camera moves close to Thorpe and the men just around him. Very quietly Thorpe is working with the dagger at the base of the chain staple.

181.   CLOSE SHOT   AT CHAIN STAPLE
The dagger, in Thorpe's hands, is digging swiftly at the wood around the staple. It is almost three quarters uncovered from the hole in the beam.

182.   MED. CLOSE SHOT   THORPE AND CARL
Carl leans backward and takes hold of the dagger with Thorpe. They strain with all their might, trying to work it free, but it doesn't budge. The dagger slips out of the crack with a scraping sound. Both men straighten, look fearfully forward.

183.   MED. SHOT   AT THE SOUND MALLET   FORWARD
The lone watch is sitting against an upright post, dozing. His breathing is regular and he shows no signs of waking.

184.   MED. SHOT   AT THORPE'S OAR
Thorpe, Abbott, Eli, and in front of them Carl and the others are pretending to sleep in case the guard heard the sound, but are actually waiting tensely. Thorpe bends down and starts digging again.

185.   CLOSE SHOT   CHAIN STAPLE
as the dagger gouges out some more splinters.

186.   MED. CLOSE SHOT   THORPE AND MEN
as he turns and nudges them, indicating for them to pull. They all reach down.

187.   MED. CLOSE SHOT   AT FLOOR ALONG CHAIN
as their hands all come into scene, taking hold of the chain which runs through their ankle irons, and strain with all their might.

188.   MED. CLOSE SHOT   AT STAPLE
as Carl and Thorpe add their strength, wrenching at it.
It pulls free.

189.   CLOSE SHOT   AT OAR
as the men wait, motionless and tense, looking around.
Thorpe bends swiftly down again.

190.   MED. CLOSE SHOT   AT FLOOR ALONG CHAIN
as Thorpe's hands take the end of the chain off the
staple and pull it cautiously through the ring on his
ankle iron. The others pull it along through theirs, taking care that it doesn't clink any more than necessary.

191.   MED. CLOSE SHOT   THE MEN
Thorpe whispers to Scott. The men move from this
point on with the grim swiftness of those who know
their lives depend on speed and precision.

THORPE:
        Under the seats, Scott . . . take care of that guard
        . . . (Scott swiftly disappears under seats, crawl-
        ing. Thorpe speaks to Abbott.) Pass the word . . .
        everyone awake . . . but pretend to sleep . . . one
        man off each seat to help . . . the others spread out
        so he won't be missed. (He slides under the seats.)

192.   CLOSE SHOT   THE GUARD
as he leans against the upright post, dozing. Scott's arm
snakes surely into scene from behind, around his throat,
pulling him back against the pillar like an iron band,
choking him into unconsciousness.

193.   MED. CLOSE SHOT   AT POST
There is a grim smile of satisfaction on Scott's face as he
relaxes his arm. The guard starts to topple. Scott plants
him firmly upright against the post and slips back into
the shadows.

194. MED. CLOSE SHOT   CARL AND THORPE
Thorpe is half under the seat. A long iron bar is through the staple. Thorpe, Carl, and four or five others are pulling on it.[32] The leverage is terrific, and the staple pulls out. The chain gives a slight clank. They freeze into immobility, Thorpe under the seat, Carl leaning against the runway wall, pretending to be asleep.

195. MED. CLOSE SHOT   DECK OF GALLEASS
A soldier on watch, who is standing with his head turned toward the rail listening, crosses to the hatchway, leading to the hold. He looks down.

196. AT HATCH
with stairway leading down into galley. At the post he sees the back of the guard at his post, apparently on watch.

197. MED. CLOSE SHOT   THE GUARD ON THE GALLEASS
The guard stands an instant longer, then strolls away, satisfied that everything is in order down below.

198. CLOSE SHOT   CARL
as one eye opens to a wary slit, grim relief in his face, and he sits up.

199. MED. CLOSE SHOT   AT CARL'S OAR
As the men pull the chain through Carl slips down under the seats and heads away with Thorpe.

200. MED. SHOT   AT TWO OARS
As the message spreads we see nudges, whispers, and eyes opening.

201. CLOSE SHOT   ANOTHER STAPLE
as it is pried out with an iron bar.

202. MED. CLOSE   ALONG CHAIN
as it is pulled through ankle irons.

203. CLOSE SHOT   SCOTT
As he tugs at another bar he looks off scene with vexation and hurries swiftly off scene.

204. MED. SHOT   THE GUARD   NIGHT
The guard is beginning to stir. As Scott comes into scene the guard's eyes open and he starts to sit up in alarm. Scott clips him on the chin with a short jolt that travels about four inches, and the guard sags back against the pillar. Scott, with a grim nod of "that will hold you," moves swiftly off scene.

205. MED. SHOT   GALLEY FLOOR   NIGHT
under benches, as two last chains are being pulled through the leg irons of the twelve men.

206. MED. SHOT   ELI   BETWEEN THE BENCHES   NIGHT
He is now on the other side of the galley. He rises cautiously and looks across the runway at Thorpe, nods to signal that all are free.

207. LONG SHOT   THE HOLD   NIGHT
Thorpe on the runway, with the released slaves clustered around him. In whispers inaudible to us, he gives the huddled men instructions. They break up. With Thorpe in the lead, they turn and steal silently up the stairs.

208. MED. LONG SHOT   MAIN DECK OF THE GALLEY   NIGHT
Three guards are stationed on the deck. One is near the hatch but looking in the opposite direction; the others are leaning against the starboard rail. Slowly the head of Thorpe appears in the hatch. He mounts to the deck with the others behind him. Silently they close in on the first guard, who is totally unaware of their approach.

Two other groups of four turn toward the guards on the starboard rail. Thorpe waits until each of the groups is directly in back of its unsuspecting victim. At a move from Thorpe the guards are jumped simultaneously and quickly overpowered, without a chance to resist or cry out.

Leaving two men to bind and gag the victims, Thorpe motions the rest of his followers toward the rail alongside the *Madre de Dios*. They crouch low in order not to be observed by the guards on the other ship. When they reach the starboard cannon, they pull back the guns so that they can slip through the openings.

CUT TO:

209. CAMERA SETUP FROM BELOW   SHOOTING UP IN
     BETWEEN THE TWO BOATS   NIGHT
We see the ropes that hold the two boats together. In the holes where the guns have stood, we see alongside the galley boat Thorpe and his various men appear, catch hold of the ropes, and monkey their way over to the other boat, hanging by their hands.

CUT TO:

210. DECK OF MADRE DE DIOS   SHOOTING TOWARD THE
     GALLEY   NIGHT
Thorpe and several of his men jump over the railing and overpower the guards in the same manner as before. Everything is done with lightning speed and catlike stealth. Thorpe turns quickly to Carl.

THORPE (in a terse half-whisper):
> Cut the anchor rope. The wind's offshore. We'll drift some distance before it's noticed. (Carl nods. Thorpe takes a quick look around the deck and beckons several of his men, including Oliver Scott and Eli Matson and Burke.) You two follow me to the captain's quarters. The rest stand guard.

Burke nods and goes off after the others, as Thorpe turns with Scott and Eli toward the doorway under the quarterdeck.

211. PROW OF THE MADRE DE DIOS   NIGHT
We see the thick rope hanging from the boat into the
water. This rope holds the anchor. Carl and some of his
men start climbing over the rail and start cutting the
anchor rope.[33]

212. MED. SHOT   INT. CAPTAIN'S QUARTERS   NIGHT
Mendoza, Ortiz, captain of the *Madre de Dios*, and two
Spanish officers are seated around an ornate mahogany
table, on which are spread out the dispatches from the
minister of war. There are four large silver goblets and a
wine bottle on the table also. There is a door leading into
the room on either side. One of the doors is ajar.

MENDOZA:
It appears, Captain Ortiz, that you and the *Madre de
Dios* will be paying the last "official" visit to Eng-
land . . .

ORTIZ (smiles, a smile on his mouth only):
The last *friendly* visit, shall we say?

MENDOZA:
I can't say I envy you this commission, to sail alone
into the enemy's port . . .

213. OUTSIDE CAPTAIN'S CABIN AT OPEN DOOR   THORPE,
SCOTT, ELI
listening

ORTIZ'S VOICE (over scene):
It is my privilege to fetch home the ambassador,
Don Alvarez, before we strike.

214. INT. CAPTAIN'S CABIN   NIGHT

ORTIZ:
Besides, England isn't an enemy until she knows
she is.

FIRST OFFICER:
> Luckily for us, she'll only know that when the Armada appears in the channel.

MENDOZA:
> And when will that be, Captain?

ORTIZ (as he folds a parchment document):
> According to this dispatch, which I am taking to Lord Wolfingham, the Armada will sail within the year. (Looks toward the window with slight puzzlement.) Odd . . .

FIRST OFFICER:
> What is it?

ORTIZ (having found a satisfactory explanation):
> The breeze must have freshened . . . We're swinging at the anchor.

SECOND OFFICER:
> Yes, I can feel the drift . . .

MENDOZA:
> Well, we better let you turn in, Captain . . . When does the crew come aboard?

ORTIZ:
> They have leave till four . . . we sail at dawn.

MENDOZA (lifts his goblet):
> Bon voyage, Captain Ortiz . . .

The two officers drink with Mendoza. Ortiz rises.

ORTIZ:
> Thank you. But I look forward more eagerly to our next voyage to England. (He picks up his goblet.) Gentlemen, I drink to the success of the Armada!

All rise, lift their glasses.

MEN (ad lib):
> The Armada! The Armada!

They clink glasses and draw back their arms to drink.
Three of them drink. One officer stops with his arm
frozen out in front of him.

215.   CLOSE SHOT   THE GOBLET
On the shiny surface of his goblet in the lamplight is
clearly mirrored the rectangle of the open door behind
him, and framed in it several figures.

216.   MED. SHOT   THE CABIN
As the two captains and the other Spanish officer put
down their glasses, the man who has seen the reflection
of Thorpe and his men in the doorway suddenly drops
his glass in midair, makes a dive for the dispatches lying
on the table in front of Ortiz, and with them in his hand
leaps for the other door.

217.   FULL SHOT   THE CABIN
Thorpe, Scott, and Eli crash into the room; the three
Spaniards stand absolutely dumbfounded. Thorpe goes
straight through the cabin in pursuit of the fleeing
Spanish officer. He vanishes out the other door. By this
time the remaining Spanish officers reach for their
swords, but Scott and Eli overturn the table, pinning
them with it against the opposite wall, bottles and goblet flying in all directions.

218.   FULL SHOT   THE MAIN DECK AFT
As the fleeing officer dashes out of the door under the
quarterdeck, he finds himself confronted by a crowd of
slaves forward on the main deck, and races up the stairs
to the quarterdeck, yelling at the top of his lungs, in the
hope of arousing another ship.

Some of the slaves start after him, but Thorpe is ahead
of them. He comes racing out the door, pauses a second,
hears the Spaniard's yells above him.

SLAVES (ad lib):
Up the stairs! The quarterdeck! That way, Captain!

Thorpe turns, takes the stairs in great leaps.

219. MED. LONG SHOT THE QUARTERDECK
just as Thorpe reaches it and the Spanish officer
disappears up the highest stairway to the poop deck.
Camera pans with Thorpe as he takes the deck in a few
strides, the stairs in a couple of leaps.

220. MED. CLOSE SHOT THE SPANIARD RAIL'S END OF THE
POOP DECK
He looks over his shoulder, hesitates for one second,
then thrusts the packet of documents inside his doublet,
climbs up on the railing, and jumps over.

221. MED. LONG SHOT STERN OF THE GALLEASS
from angle of the water. The Spaniard is in midair. He
lands in the water with a great splash and strikes out
away from the ship. Thorpe appears on the railing,
stands up on it, makes a beautiful dive in a huge arc
hitting the water almost halfway to the Spaniard. He
starts after him with long, powerful strokes.

222. MED. CLOSE SHOT THE TWO MEN
in the water, just as Thorpe overtakes the Spanish
officer. There is a great skirmish and splashing which
we can only partly make out in the semidarkness. Once
the two men disappear completely under the water,
come up a little way apart. The officer tries to get away
again but Thorpe is on him almost at once, and it is
apparent the Spaniard is getting the worst of it. Thorpe
now grabs his head and shoves him below the surface,
holds him there. Presently the Spaniard's arm comes
out of the water, the packet clutched in his hand, sur-
rendering them to Thorpe to save his life. Thorpe takes
the packet, releases the officer, and starts back to the
galleass.[34]

DISSOLVE TO:

223. MED. SHOT   RAIL OF SHIP
Scott and Carl are waiting. Thorpe appears out of the darkness, swims to the ship. Scott and Carl pull him up on the ladder, which doesn't quite reach the water.

THORPE (panting):
> They may have heard us on shore! Cut loose the galley . . . break out sails . . . out of the harbor, quick!

SCOTT:
> Aye, Cap'n.[35]

224. MED. LONG SHOT   WAIST OF THE GALLEASS
Scott climbing over the rail to the deck as the waiting men crowd around him. There is the sound of a single cannon shot from off scene.

SCOTT:
> Under weigh, lads . . . they've spotted us! . . . Abbott, take two men and cut loose the galley . . . Burke, you take the lookout . . . the rest of you into the rigging . . . break out every last sail . . . Lawson and Peters, help Mr. Pitt man the guns.

VOICES (ad lib):
> Aye, sir . . . Aye . . . Aye, mate . . .

The men break swiftly into groups, part of them rush to the mainmast and start climbing, others run fore and aft.

SCOTT:
> Eli, set the course. Keep her hard alee.

ELI:
> Aye.

There are two heavy booms from off scene.

CARL:
> Come on, me lads! Give the Spaniards a taste of their own powder!

They spring to the nearest cannon on the port side. (NOTE: Stock shots from *Captain Blood* are suitable for the following battle in the harbor of Cádiz, and the escape of Thorpe and his men aboard the captured ship.)

225. FULL SHOT   THE HARBOR   (STOCK)   NIGHT
firing of guns at different points along the shore.

226. FULL SHOT   THE MADRE DE DIOS   (MINIATURE)
returning the Spanish fire with its port guns flashing in the night.

227. MED. SHOT   THORPE
still breathing heavily, leans back against the quarter-deck rail, looking up at the rigging, checking the progress of the sailors.

228. ANGLE SHOT   OF THE RIGGING
Men swinging like monkeys; white sails breaking out swiftly against the night sky; continuous roar of cannon off scene.

229. MED. SHOT   MAIN DECK OF THE MADRE DE DIOS
Amid a bedlam of noise, men are bringing up powder and balls from the hold through the hatch. Pan to the port rail. At Carl's signal, Peters sets off a cannon pointed to the shore. Camera pans along the rail as other cannons are discharged at the Spanish city. (Last cut will be taken from stock.)

230. FULL SHOT   THE SHORE   (STOCK)
Flashes of guns. The reports more distant now.

231. MED. SHOT   THORPE AT QUARTERDECK RAIL
looking out toward the shore. Guns are fading out. Carl and Scott come running up.
SCOTT:
    We're out of their range, Cap'n.

THORPE:
> Good work.

CARL:
> And with that offshore breeze we'll be out of this
> harbor in the twinkling of a bedpost.

THORPE:
> As soon as we're out, bear off the coast and head for
> Dover.

SCOTT:
> Dover . . .

They are all silent for a moment.

CARL (breaking the silence):
> Cap'n, I knew something was wrong, all during
> that fight. Look . . . we're flying the Spanish flag.

SCOTT:
> Shall I have her hauled down, Cap'n?

THORPE:
> Leave her up. (Grimly.) Sea Hawks aren't welcome
> in England. Philip's flag will give us safe conduct.
> (Significantly; taps the packet of papers.) Besides,
> His Excellency, Don Alvarez, is expecting a *Spanish*
> ship.

They smile at each other as we

FADE OUT

FADE IN

232.   FULL SHOT   LONDON GATE   NIGHT
A coach has just been examined and drives out of shot.
The coach of Don Alvarez now rides up. An officer steps
forward in routine fashion. Coach stops.

233.   MED. SHOT   COACH   AT LONDON GATE
Window is let down. Don Alvarez appears in the opening. In the background Maria can be seen.

OFFICER:
>   Your passport, please.

ALVAREZ:
>   Here. (Hands credentials to the officer who examines them briefly.)

OFFICER (touches his hat):
>   Very well, Your Excellency. Sorry to have stopped you. We're taking precautions about the privateers, sir.

ALVAREZ:
>   I understand.

Window shuts. Guards move off.[36]

>   DISSOLVE TO:

234.   INT. OF COACH   CLOSE TWO-SHOT   ALVAREZ AND
MARIA   NIGHT
They are inside a coach, which jogs along at a brisk pace. Outside there is a thick fog which shuts off any views through the windows.

ALVAREZ:
>   Maria, there is still time to reconsider. I can hold the boat at Dover while we send for your things.

MARIA (firmly):
>   No, Uncle, I shall stay here. I feel more at home.

ALVAREZ:
>   But if trouble should come between our country and England, your position here may become very difficult.

MARIA:
>   After all, I'm as much English as Spanish . . . (Significantly.) Perhaps more.

ALVAREZ:
>   Is that the reason, Maria?

MARIA:

> I can't return to Spain as long as there's any hope of
> . . . Uncle, let's not talk of it anymore. I shall be
> lonely and homesick—yes. But now I should be
> lonely wherever I am.

Alvarez looks at her with pity and understanding, and
they both look ahead of them silently as we

DISSOLVE TO:

235. FULL SHOT SHORE OF DOVER   NIGHT

A small pinnace nears the strand. Several of its rowers
jump into the water, pull the small boat up on the misty
shore. Camera pulls up to show Thorpe, dressed in the
uniform of a Spanish officer, alighting from the boat. He
turns toward the men who stay in the pinnace.

THORPE:

> Abbott, you're in charge of the boat. When Don
> Alvarez comes, talk to him in Spanish. Tell him
> you're taking him to Captain Ortiz.

ABBOTT:

> What shall we do when we get him on board?

THORPE:

> Hold him until further orders.

ABBOTT:

> And what about you, Captain? How will you get to
> the queen?

THORPE (briefly):
> I'll take care of that.

MEN (ad lib):
> Aye, Cap'n. Good luck, Cap'n. Good luck. Etc.

With a wave of his arm Thorpe turns and is off.

DISSOLVE TO:

236.   CLOSE SHOT   THORPE   NIGHT
along a wall, looking intently off scene through the drift-
ing mist.

237.   FULL SHOT   DOVER SHORE   NIGHT
We see a coach with four horses, two figures on the
coachman's box. Toward the water's edge we see the
figures of Alvarez and Maria as they approach the waiting pinnace, which now has a large chest in its stern. A
figure (Abbott) steps up, bows, says something not audible to us; Alvarez embraces his niece, then boards the
pinnace, assisted by Abbott. The oars dip in the water;
from his seat in the prow Alvarez waves goodbye to his
niece, who flutters her handkerchief. The small boat
quickly melts into the fog. (Be sure that balance of
oarsmen are none of Thorpe's previous crew which may
be recognized by Alvarez.)

238.   MED. LONG SHOT   THE COACH
its horses restless and prancing. One of the figures
above sees Maria returning, comes down from the box,
and goes to assist her into the coach.

239.   MED. CLOSE SHOT   INT. OF THE COACH   NIGHT
Maria enters, starts as she sees a man sitting in the other
corner, then suddenly recognizes him. Thorpe claps a
hand over her mouth before she can utter a cry. He
gestures up toward the box of the coach. The vehicle
now starts with a noisy clatter, and Thorpe slowly
draws back his hand.

THORPE:
I'm sorry. I was afraid you might cry out.

240.   CLOSE SHOT   MARIA
trying to convince herself that it is actually Thorpe sitting beside her.

241.   MARIA AND THORPE

Thorpe, interpreting her silence as a carry-over of the old pride, tries to explain.

THORPE:
I have to reach London. I saw your coach waiting. There was nothing else I could do . . .

MARIA (weakly, beginning to find her voice):
Where did you come from? How did you get here?

THORPE:
On the boat that came for your uncle. (Suddenly wonders.) Why didn't you go with him?

MARIA (as if explaining everything):
He's going to Spain . . .

THORPE (a flicker of a smile):
He is . . . ? And you're staying here? (Maria can only nod.) Why?

Maria slowly raises her head until her face is close to his. Then she speaks with a desperate rush of words.

MARIA:
Don't you know why? Don't you know that I . . . I love you? . . . That I've loved you ever since that day in the rose garden? Oh, I kept it from you then. I was too proud. But I'm not proud anymore. Ever since you went away, I've been in torment thinking something might happen to you . . . and you'd never know. And then it *did* happen, and I've never forgiven myself until . . . now. Only, I can't believe that I've found you again.

During this confession, Thorpe has just looked at her, trying to realize the actuality of what he hears. There are tears in her eyes when she finishes. Then she deliberately covers her emotion with pretended concern over his failure to respond.

MARIA:

> Geoffrey, won't you . . . say something, please?
> You just look at me as if . . .

THORPE:

> I'm sorry . . . I—I can't realize yet.

MARIA (looks at him searchingly):

> You do care for me still?

THORPE:

> Maria, there were times in Panama and the galley
> when I'd have given my life for just one more look
> at you. Now you're here sitting close to me, and
> . . . and I still can't believe it's true.

MARIA:

> Put your arms around me . . . (He obeys mechani-
> cally.) No, tighter . . . (He draws her to him.)
> There, you see I'm not a ghost . . . I'm here and
> we're together and nothing is ever going to separate
> us again. Not distance, not pride . . . not even a
> large bouquet of English roses.[37]

They both laugh and now the strangeness between
them is dissipated.

THORPE:

> Maria, I've lived all my life on the sea. I haven't
> much to offer you . . . (Somewhat ruefully.) A cap-
> tain without a ship—

MARIA:

> I might have been jealous of your ship. You loved
> her, didn't you?

THORPE (looks at her tenderly):

> She was my *first* love.

She smiles yes to the implied meaning in his words. He
draws her face to his and they kiss.

DISSOLVE TO:

241A.   MED. SHOT CAPTAIN'S CABIN   NIGHT
(Same as previous scene with Ortiz, Mendoza, etc.)
Standing before a small wall mirror, Carl is putting on
the coat to his Spanish lieutenant's uniform. Being a
larger man than its previous owner, Carl has to pull on it
to get it buttoned. He is giving himself an admiring
glance in the mirror when there is a knock at the door.
Quickly Carl drops in the chair behind the desk and
pretends to study some papers.

CARL (in an uncertain accent):
   Adelante. (Come in.)

Alvarez enters the doorway with Abbott just behind
him. Carl's head is still bent over the papers so that the
Spanish ambassador cannot see his face. Alvarez waits a
moment for "Captain Ortiz" to recognize and greet him,
then gives a slight cough but even this fails to attract
Carl's attention. The perplexed Spaniard glances
around at Abbott, who is seemingly unaware of anything unusual in the situation. Finally Alvarez can restrain himself no longer.

ALVAREZ (indignantly):
   Captain Ortiz! (At this, Carl's head comes up and
   he beams on the astounded Alvarez who, at first,
   can only stare at him.) You! What are you doing
   here? Where is Captain Ortiz?

CARL:
   Well, the last time I saw him, señor, he was swim-
   ming in the harbor of Cádiz.

ALVAREZ (turns furiously on Abbott):
   Take me off this boat! I shall protest to the queen! I
   shall demand passage to Spain!

CARL (dryly):
   Your Excellency, I'm afraid you'll have to wait until
   the war's over. Cap'n Thorpe said to make you
   comfortable because it might last quite a little time.

ALVAREZ (shaken as the truth dawns on him):
Captain Thorpe? But . . . he's a prisoner.

CARL (grimly):
That's where you're wrong, Don Alvarez. You're *his* prisoner.

DISSOLVE TO:

242.   THE FOLLOWING SHOTS:
The wheels of the coach on the uneven road, from the side. They dip into a rut, splash some muddy water out, roll over some small stones, and on;
The horses' hooves, from the side—eight pairs of them, moving briskly, picking up their feet. They spin out a stone occasionally, splash through a puddle;
The box of the coach. The two men jogging along silently, looking forward. Presently the coachman speaks without turning his head.

COACHMAN:
Curse this fog. It'll be late before we're in London.

The other pays no attention to the remark, continues to stare off scene forward. Camera moves close to his face. It is the spy, Kroner.

243.   MED. SHOT   THORPE AND MARIA   INSIDE THE COACH
They sit silently, Thorpe holding both Maria's hands in her lap. They give the impression of having ridden this way—blissfully—for hours. Finally Maria looks up at him.

MARIA:
Geoffrey, I'm so happy, I . . . I'm frightened. (He smiles reassuringly at her.) But you *are* in danger
. . .

THORPE:
That'll be over once I reach the queen.

MARIA (worried):
But they're stopping everyone at London gate.

THORPE (ruefully):
> Looking for honest English sailors. Well, this Spanish uniform should be in my favor.

MARIA (after a pause):
> It's strange, but it never occurs to me anymore that I'm Spanish and you're English. That doesn't seem important.

THORPE:
> It isn't.

MARIA:
> I know nothing of politics and war—but I believe in you, and whatever you do must be the right thing . . . Please let me help you.

THORPE:
> If I can only get in the castle without being recognized.

MARIA:
> I'll take you in my entrance. Miss Latham's waiting up to let me in.

THORPE (glances up toward the box):
> What about them . . . when they see me step out?

MARIA:
> I'll tell them I'm smuggling in my lover. (They both laugh. She again presses her head against his shoulder.) After all, it's the truth!

>> DISSOLVE TO:

244. FULL SHOT   EXT. WALL AND GATES OF LONDON   NIGHT
The gate is heavily guarded by a dozen men-at-arms under an officer. They are halting every vehicle which passes through the gate; at one side soldiers are stopping pedestrians, making them remove their hats, scrutinizing them, searching them under the light of torches.

245.   MED. SHOT   THE GATE
Maria's coach comes up, stops.

OFFICER (holds his hand up toward the box):
    Your pass . . .

KRONER (leans in front of the coachman to address the
officer, calls down):
    We passed through this morning taking His Excel-
    lency, the Spanish ambassador, to Dover. (With a
    nod back.) Only his niece inside . . .

OFFICER:
    Can you identify yourselves?

The coachman and Kroner both reach into their dou-
blets.
                                        CUT TO:

246.   MED. SHOT   INT. OF THE COACH
The shades are all pulled down. Maria and Thorpe are
waiting tensely in the dark coach.

MARIA (whispers):
    Something's the matter. We're stopping so long.

Thorpe doesn't speak. Maria sits forward on the seat,
Thorpe hunched back in the far corner. The door on
Maria's side opens. We can dimly see the officer outside.

OFFICER:
    I beg your pardon, my lady, I'll have to ask you to
    identify yourself.

MARIA (nervously):
    Certainly . . .

She reaches into an embroidered bag and starts to take
out some papers. The officer leans in the coach a little
way to reach for them, and as he does so, sees Thorpe.

OFFICER (taking Maria's papers):
    They told me outside you were alone . . . I'll have
    to see your papers too, sir.

THORPE (as low a voice as possible):
> Officer, I just came in on the *Madre de Dios* . . . I
> wasn't expecting to go to London.

OFFICER:
> Well, look here, now . . . I can't let . . .

MARIA (interrupting):
> It was my uncle, Don Alvarez, who sent him,
> officer—a special mission . . .

OFFICER (stubbornly):
> I'm sorry, lady, but my orders are no one goes
> through this gate without a pass or . . .

THORPE (a sudden inspiration, reaching into his doublet
for one of the dispatches):
> An important dispatch for Lord Wolfingham,
> officer . . .

The officer looks at the dispatch addressed to
Wolfingham.

CUT TO:

247.   MED. SHOT   INT. THE COACH

OFFICER (receding):
> Very well, then . . . sorry to have delayed you.

He slams the coach door and Maria turns with tremendous relief to Thorpe; but he is looking up toward the
slit in the front of the coach, transfixed.[38]

248.   CLOSE SHOT   KRONER'S FACE
Through the slit, Thorpe's angle. There is recognition
and menace in the narrow eyes.

249.   MED. SHOT   INT. THE COACH
The coach starts moving. Thorpe is looking straight up
at the narrow slit, seeing part of Kroner's face. He has
seen his face somewhere before and is trying to place it.

CUT TO:

250. MED. SHOT THE BOX OF THE COACH

KRONER (flatly; to the coachman):
When we get inside the grounds, drive straight to the guardhouse at the main entrance, and drive fast.

DRIVER:
But her ladyship . . .

KRONER (emphatically):
The main entrance.

DISSOLVE TO:

251. INT. COACH

Maria and Thorpe sit silently. Presumably they have heard the instructions Kroner has given. The coach is moving at high speed now, causing a great deal of motion inside. Thorpe and Maria are hurriedly unfastening the canvas flap at the back of the coach. Through the opening we can see only darkness and rolling mist. He turns to Maria, who now looks very frightened.

MARIA:
They're going so fast . . .

THORPE:
I'll be all right. Don't be afraid.

MARIA:
Francis, darling . . .

He takes her quickly into his arms, kisses her, then climbs to the opening in the rear of the coach.

MARIA (wild-eyed):
Two knocks, remember . . . oh, no, it's too high—don't!

But Thorpe has sprung through the aperture and disappeared into the night.

252. MED. LONG SHOT   REAR OF COACH
traveling away from camera at full speed. A figure hur-
tles out of the rear, lands on his feet, but rolls over and
over. The coach quickly melts into the darkness. Thorpe
picks himself up, cautiously starts towards a lamplit
doorway which is a private entrance to the castle.

253. FULL SHOT   THE COACH
pulling up to the main entrance to the castle. A lieutenant of the guards steps out. Several soldiers are behind
him.

254. MED. SHOT   THE COACH
as it comes to a stop in front of the guardhouse.

KRONER (shouts down):
Lieutenant, in the coach! Captain Thorpe . . . Arrest him!

As Kroner starts down from the box the soldiers
converge on the two sides of the coach. The lieutenant
springs to the door on his side, flings it open. The camera pulls up to show the seat which is occupied only by
Maria, who steps out looking with feigned astonish-
ment at the lieutenant's drawn sword.

MARIA (with great show of innocence):
Am I in some danger, Lieutenant?

LIEUTENANT (puzzled; his sword drops):
Your pardon, Doña Maria, I . . . I thought . . .

KRONER (comes rushing up to them):
What's the trouble, Lieutenant? Where is he?

LIEUTENANT (believing he is the victim of a joke and
resenting it):
You should know that better than I.

KRONER (his turn to be amazed):
But he was in there when we entered the castle gate
. . . Doña Maria, where's Captain Thorpe?

MARIA:

> Captain Thorpe? (She looks at the lieutenant as if to inquire whether Kroner is in his right mind.) Mr. Kroner, I don't know what you're talking about. (She walks out of shot.)

KRONER:

> Lieutenant, I want you to station guards at all entrances leading to the queen, and order an immediate search of the castle grounds.

LIEUTENANT (demurring):

> By whose authority, Mr. Kroner?

KRONER:

> Lord Wolfingham's. You'll have his written order as soon as I can get to him. Now hurry.[39]

LIEUTENANT (still unconvinced):

> But Doña Maria said . . .

KRONER (breaking in):

> I tell you Thorpe was in the carriage. She was protecting him.

They both turn, look off scene. Camera pulls back to include the waiting soldiers and the coach, but Maria has disappeared.

LIEUTENANT (to his men):

> Where did she go?

SERGEANT:

> Her ladyship went into the castle, Lieutenant.

LIEUTENANT (caustically):

> Sergeant, order out four squads of the castle guards. Take one of them to the other door and search Doña Maria's apartment.

SERGEANT (salutes):

> Yes, sir. (He turns on his heel.)

CUT TO:

255. MED. SHOT   SITTING ROOM OF MARIA'S APARTMENT
looking toward the door which leads out to the hall. We
hear two knocks of a heavy knocker on a door off below,
then a pause and another two knocks. Miss Latham, in a
dressing gown, carrying a candle, comes into the shot.
She crosses to the apartment door, which she unlatches
and walks through.

256. MED. SHOT   MISS LATHAM
descending a narrow stone staircase, the candlelight
flickering on either wall. She reaches the bottom where
there is a heavy outside door, as the two knocks are
repeated.

MISS LATHAM:
   One moment, Maria . . .

She slips a heavy bolt and the door pushes open.
Thorpe stands before her in the dark doorway. Miss
Latham is rooted in amazement as Thorpe slips in
quickly, bolting the door behind him.

MISS LATHAM:
   Captain Thorpe!

THORPE:
   Not here . . . upstairs . . .

They start up the same stairway, Miss Latham in the
lead, carrying the candle.

257. MED. SHOT   MARIA'S SITTING ROOM
Miss Latham and Thorpe enter silently. He closes the
door behind them, carefully latches it.

MISS LATHAM:
   Why, Captain Thorpe, how on earth did you get
   here? We thought . . .

THORPE:
   Yes, I know. I saw Maria.

MISS LATHAM:
Where is she?

THORPE:
At the castle entrance. She said I could depend on
you.

MISS LATHAM:
Captain Thorpe, are you in danger?

THORPE:
Until I get to the queen.

MISS LATHAM (after a moment's pause she decides to
trust him):
I'll help you. There is a private corridor to the queen
. . .

THORPE:
Good.

MISS LATHAM:
Oh, Captain Thorpe . . . (Somewhat hesitantly.)
Did that . . . er, uh . . . did Carl come back?

THORPE (smiles):
Carl always comes back. He's at Dover.

She looks relieved. Just as they start toward the rear of
the room, there is a brusque knock on the door by which
they entered. They both turn.

MISS LATHAM (whispers):
The door straight ahead. Then the first corridor to
your left.

THORPE:
Hold them as long as you can.

She nods. He moves out of the shot. She turns back
toward the apartment door, where the raps are now
more insistent.

MISS LATHAM (through the door):
Well, what do you want?

VOICE OF SERGEANT (off scene):
We have an order to search your rooms.

MISS LATHAM:
Search our rooms? What on earth for?

VOICE OF SERGEANT (off scene):
Lady, I'm sorry, but I can't take time to explain.
Either you open that door or we break it in.

MISS LATHAM:
Break in that door and the queen will hear of it.

VOICE OF SERGEANT (off scene):
The queen will hear of it if we don't.

MISS LATHAM:
Very well, then . . . break it in.

She takes a seat near the light, reaches her work basket,
and calmly begins to crochet as the soldiers outside start
to batter down the door, which will obviously keep
them busy for a few minutes.

258. MED. SHOT HALLWAY
where Thorpe makes his way, keeping close to the inside wall. Directly ahead of him is a lighted area under
burning candles. He runs quickly through this into the
shadows beyond. He pauses at an intersecting corridor,
looks cautiously around the corner.

259. FULL SHOT CORRIDOR
looking toward a doorway (from Thorpe's angle). Two
sentries guard the door. Thorpe turns back the way he
came.

260. FULL SHOT THE FIRST HALLWAY
in reverse direction. Four figures with burning torches
suddenly appear ahead of Thorpe. He turns, runs to-

ward the camera and off scene. The oncoming guards
see him, raise a shout, and start in pursuit.

261.   MED. LONG SHOT   A MAIN HALLWAY
much wider than the other, suits of armor on pedestals,
doors opening off. Two soldiers stand on guard outside
one of the doors. Thorpe dashes around the corner almost in the arms of the sentries. He draws his sword,
engages them, is driving them back and away from the
door in a fierce attack when the pursuing guards round
the corner to join the sentries. At the same time more
soldiers, attracted by the noise of the fight, appear from
other doorways, and the huge hall is now alive with
glowing torches. As the reinforcements converge on
Thorpe, he upsets a suit of armor in their path, and in
their moment of confusion he turns and bolts through
the doorway in back of them.

262.   FULL SHOT   NARROW CORRIDOR
Thorpe running toward a huge door, a horde of guards
after them. He swings the door open, then closes it from
the other side in the faces of the pursuing soldiers, who
throw their weight against the door.

263.   CLOSE SHOT   THORPE
Bolting the door from the other side. He leans back
against the door for a moment to get his breath, then
turns slowly around. His look of momentary relief
changes to dismay.

WOLFINGHAM'S VOICE (over scene):
    Have you nine lives, Captain Thorpe?

264.   MED. LONG SHOT   THE PRIVATE AUDIENCE ROOM
of Lord Wolfingham, illuminated by candles burning in
niches in each of the four walls. There are doors on
either end of the room. Behind a massive desk stands
Wolfingham, smiling at Thorpe with perfect composure.

WOLFINGHAM:
Surely by now most of them must be used up.

On the door behind Thorpe the pounding of the guards becomes more threatening. Thorpe's eyes dart to the door on the opposite side of the room. Wolfingham reads his glance and draws his sword.

WOLFINGHAM:
I'm afraid I shall have to ask you not to disturb Her Highness.

Suddenly Thorpe springs across the room toward the opposite door but Wolfingham is there before him. They cross swords, attack and parry with savage brilliance.

WOLFINGHAM (as they duel):
I was expecting you, Captain . . . but not in a Spanish uniform.

THORPE (significantly):
You should be wearing it.

WOLFINGHAM (smiling):
Perhaps I shall . . . one day.

Thorpe launches a furious attack, edging his opponent away from the queen's door. Thorpe gets his hand on the latch, but Wolfingham's counterattack presses him back before he can open it. By now the door in the rear of the room is groaning under the terrific battering of the guards.

WOLFINGHAM:
You won't be so lucky this time . . . . as Panama.[40]

THORPE:
I lost most of my men there . . . thanks to you.

Thorpe is now deliberately retreating around the sides of the room. As he passes the lighted candles in the wall niches he watches his chance to slash at the candles with a side stroke of his sword. The room darkens gradually as the candles are extinguished until only one dim flame is left. As he becomes aware of Thorpe's desperate strategy Wolfingham retreats to protect the last candle.

WOLFINGHAM:
> One light you won't put out, Captain . . .

THORPE:
> A traitor should be at home in the dark.

Taking advantage of his opponent's retreat, Thorpe suddenly veers toward the queen's door, gets his back to it, reaches for the latch, but Wolfingham is on him again with frantic strokes.[41]

At this instant the other door gives way with a splintering crash, and the castle guards pour in the dimly lit room. Wolfingham relaxes his guard for a brief moment, and Thorpe plunges his sword through his opponent's body. Wolfingham drops at the feet of the charging soldiers, who converge on Thorpe.

He fends them off with his last strength, but they press him back against the door. A dozen soldiers are ready to pierce him when the heavy door swings open and Elizabeth stands imperiously, silhouetted in the lighted doorway, a guard on either side of her, Maria slightly behind. The soldiers pause. Their swords gradually lower under the queen's gaze. Thorpe is bleeding, disheveled, exhausted. He turns toward Elizabeth, his sword dropping from his hand as he falls to one knee. He reaches in his doublet, pulls out the dispatches, hands them to the queen.

THORPE:
> Your Grace . . . secret dispatches from Spain to Wolfingham . . . proof of their plans to send the Armada against England.

As Elizabeth receives the documents, we
DISSOLVE TO:

265. FULL SHOT QUARTERDECK OF AN ENGLISH SHIP
in Dover harbor. (*Albatross* can be used without showing
her name.) Queen Elizabeth is knighting Thorpe before
a large assemblage of court dignitaries and naval
officers. Sailors are aloft in the rigging to get a view of
the ceremony.[42]

266. MED. SHOT QUARTERDECK ELIZABETH, THORPE, AND
PART OF ASSEMBLAGE
Thorpe kneeling before the queen. A sword in her hand
rests on his shoulder. In the front row back of Thorpe
stand the Sea Hawks: Hawkins, Frobisher, etc., and also
Carl, Tom, and Eli, and all other survivors, all dressed
up for the occasion and standing at attention with up-
raised swords. On the queen's right is Sir John Burleson, proud and beaming. Other members of the council
are in back, maids of honor and other attendants to one
side.

ELIZABETH:

    Stand, Sir Francis Thorpe. (He rises. She hands him
    the sword—hilt first—with which she knighted
    him.) Accept by my hand the homage of your
    country, and the gratitude of its queen.

Thorpe thrusts the sword in its scabbard, bows low,
reverently kisses the outstretched hand of the queen.
Camera pans over the assemblage, now breaking into
loud applause, then comes to rest for a moment on
Maria, among the maids of honor, her face uplifted and
radiant. The camera follows her eyes around to Thorpe,
who steps back into an end position in the row of Sea
Hawks. Camera pans over the faces of these men until it
rests on Carl, who grins happily as he glances off scene
to his left. Camera follows his gaze to Miss Latham, who
smiles but drops her eyes as an English lady should.

267. MED. SHOT   QUEEN AND ASSEMBLAGE

ELIZABETH:

> And now, my loyal subjects, a grave duty confronts
> us all . . . to prepare our nation for a war that none
> of us wants—least of all your queen. We have tried
> by all means within our power to avert this conflict.
> We have no quarrel with the people of Spain . . .

Camera pulls up to a close shot of Thorpe, who turns his
head slightly in Maria's direction. His expression reveals
his love for her and asks for affirmation. [Camera pulls
up to a] close shot of Maria. She smiles very slightly and
nods in answer to his look.

ELIZABETH'S VOICE (over scene):

> . . . or of any other country. But when the ruthless
> ambitions of a man threaten to engulf the world, it
> becomes the solemn obligation of free men, wher-
> ever they may be, to affirm that the earth belongs
> not to any man, but to all men . . .

268. MED. SHOT   ELIZABETH AND ASSEMBLAGE

ELIZABETH (continuing):

> . . . and that freedom is the deed and title to the
> soil on which we exist. Firm in this faith, we shall
> now make ready to meet the great Armada which
> Philip sends against us. To this end I pledge you
> ships worthy of our seamen . . . a sturdy fleet
> hewn out of the forests of England. (Camera pans
> to the wooded shore that surrounds the harbor, and
> as we look, each tall pine becomes a ship's lofty
> spar—row upon row of them—a forest of mast-
> heads, and each flying the British flag. Elizabeth's
> voice continues over scene.) A navy foremost in the
> world—not only in our time, but in generations to
> come.

The wooden masts

DISSOLVE TO:

269. THE STEEL SUPERSTRUCTURE OF MODERN WARSHIPS
A martial anthem swells over the queen's voice. On a
full shot of Britain's battle fleet in majestic parade[43] we

FADE OUT

THE END

Notes to the Screenplay

Although the script is dated January 30, 1940, and marked Second Revised Final, it does contain changes that were made later during filming, but before photography of the modified scenes (the last revisions are marked March 23, 1940). The screenplay is "as written," however, not "as filmed," so that one is able to analyze the evolution from script to edited film.

1 The foreword was omitted on the screen at the request of Warners' New York legal department because of possible complications regarding Louis Parker's play, *Drake* (see Introduction).

2 King Philip II (see figure 1), King of Spain (1556–98), King of Naples and Sicily (1554–98), and King of Portugal (1580–98). In 1558, Philip proposed marriage to Queen Elizabeth I of England, but he was refused. His bureaucratic absolutism inevitably caused discontent.

3 The galleass was an improved outgrowth of the oared galley, which was unseaworthy and lacked endurance because of its necessary lightness. The galleass mounted a few guns on the broadside in addition to the fore and aft guns that were common to the galley.

4 In all of the earlier drafts of the script, Thorpe's ship was called the *Falcon*, but in early December of 1939 Jack L. Warner asked that another name be found because the *Falcon* had been used in Paramount's *Rulers of the Sea* (1939). Writer Howard Koch suggested *Albatross*, a bird of vengeance and superstition of the seas.

5 Various drafts of the scripts alternated between "Francis Thorpe" and "Geoffrey Thorpe." Shortly after filming began the Warners' New York legal department requested that "Geoffrey" be used.

6 A few shots from the 1935 *Captain Blood* and the 1929 *Divine Lady* were interspersed with newly filmed battle material (figures 3 and 4).

7 The ship miniatures were built and photographed for this picture (figure 2).

8 The entire sea battle as shot and edited is considerably more detailed than the script indicates. Director Michael Curtiz staged what certainly can be regarded as one of the most elaborate sequences of its kind.

9 Historically, there were no "sea hawks." They were referred to as "sea dogs."

10 Thorpe refers to the Spanish Inquisition, the purpose of which—in theory, at least—was initially to discover and punish converted Jews (and later Muslims and Protestants) who were insincere. However, soon no Spaniard could feel safe from it. The Spanish Inquisition was entirely controlled by Spanish kings and was much harsher, more highly organized, and freer with the death penalty than the medieval Inquisition. Philip II viciously prosecuted the Inquisition in his efforts to extend the Catholic faith.

11 This scene was staged belowdecks in a cabin. (In the 1947 reissue it was eliminated.)

12 Burleson, Wolfingham, and Abbott are all fictitious characters. In fact, the only historical figures in the entire drama are Philip, Elizabeth, Sir John Hawkins, and Martin Frobisher (the latter two being "sea dogs" of the time, here represented as "sea hawks").

13 The southernmost point of Great Britain, a peninsula at Cornwall, is called Lizard Point or Lizard Head. In the film it is referred to not by name but as a promontory.

14 No chanty was used.

15 As stated earlier, Frobisher and Hawkins are historical names but the other "sea hawks" ("sea dogs") are fictitious.

16 Two Spanish ambassadors, Don Gerau de Spes and Don Bernardino de Mendoza, protested on different occasions to Queen Elizabeth the piratical acts of English seamen. According to all histories, there can be no doubt that Elizabeth, while officially at peace with Spain and trying to stay at peace, was secretly encouraging men like the sea dogs Drake, Hawkins, and Frobisher in their "trading expeditions," which degenerated at times into rank piracy. There also can be no doubt that Elizabeth officially appeased the Spanish ambassador whenever he complained, but never actually did anything to punish or even stop her sea captains from pursuing these enterprises. Thorpe's attitude toward Spain resembles that of Drake; also, in his attempts to take action against Philip by using his influence on the queen, he is patterned after Drake.

17 All of Thorpe's exposition regarding the "New World treasure" and the procedure by which it was routed is historically accurate.

18 This sequence was originally planned to be filmed at the old Busch Gardens in Pasadena but was later changed to the backlot (figure 12).

19 It is historically accurate that a great number of highly placed persons at Elizabeth's court were paid by Spain—or at least in the interests of Spain—and at least one Spanish ambassador was in-

volved in a conspiracy, consisting of the Duke of Norfolk and a great number of other noblemen who intended to restore Catholicism to England, support Mary Stuart (Mary Queen of Scots) as queen, and restore Spanish supremacy over England in general. Miller's scripts used this motivation rather than the threat of the Armada.

20 This entire scene was deleted before the picture's initial release in America, but was retained in England.

21 This line was deleted.

22 The remainder of this scene was dropped.

23 Scene 127 was deleted.

24 From scene 128D up to this point the sequence was shot and/or edited in a different manner from what is rendered in the text. For example, the explosives under the bridge were not included.

25 Changed from "jungle" to "swamp."

26 In an earlier draft, when the men reach the edge of the jungle they see that the *Albatross* is on fire. Dropping on the beach from exhaustion and hopelessness, they sleep, but are awakened and captured by the Spaniards.

27 Drake was a legend in his own lifetime. To his countrymen he was thought to be possessed of superhuman powers, derived from God. To the Spaniards he was the master of black and dire magic—"The Dragon of the Apocalypse." At that time the possession of magical powers—black and white—was implicitly accepted universally.

28 Both *Captain Blood* and *The Adventures of Robin Hood* contain similar scenes in which the character portrayed by Flynn is unjustly charged and condemned by a cruel judge or noble.

29 Maria's song:

> Stood a maiden at her window,
> Sadly gazing out to sea,
> Pale her cheek, her heart how heavy,
> Sorrowful her melody!
> "My love is far from me!"
>
> The evening yields its light,
> A star awaits the night.
>
> And the wind brings back an echo,
> Faintly from across the sea!
> Carries home her melody:
> "My love is far from me!"

(Music by Erich Wolfgang Korngold; lyric by Howard Koch.)

30 The entire montage was dropped.

31 Historically, there was a great Portuguese ship of the period called the *Madre de Dios*.

32 The iron bar was not used at any time in the filmed sequence.

33 Dropped.

34 In the film, Thorpe chases the Spanish officer to the deck where the two struggle in hand-to-hand combat. Thorpe at last is able to seize the dispatches as he knocks his opponent into the water.

35 In the film, as the ship gets under way the crew breaks into a rousing song:

> Pull on the oars,
> Freedom is yours,
> Strike for the shores of Dover;
> Over the sea,
> Hearty and free,
> Troubles will soon be over.
> Sing as you row,
> Here we go,
> For we know that we row,
> For home sweet home.
>
> Pull on the oars,
> Freedom is yours,
> Strike for the shores of Dover.
> Over the sea,
> Hearty and free,
> Troubles will soon be over,
>
> Here we go,
> For we know that we row for home!
> Sailing for home!

(Music by Erich Wolfgang Korngold; lyric by Howard Koch and Jack Scholl.)

The sequence fades out at the conclusion of the singing as the ship sails away from camera. The remainder of the scripted material up to the fade out at the end of scene 231 was not included in the final cut of the film.

36 Scenes 232 and 233 were eliminated.

37 In the film, the material from this point until the last few lines of scene 243 was deleted.

38 Scenes 244 through 247 were dropped.

39 The remainder of scene 254 was deleted.

40 All of the dialogue up to and including this line is exchanged before

the duel begins. During the fight there is no dialogue. (The next three lines were dropped.)

41 In the film, the opponents continue the duel through other rooms and passages and into the throne room.

42 On April 4, 1581, Queen Elizabeth knighted Drake on board his ship, the *Golden Hind*. Mendoza, the Spanish ambassador, was furious that this "master thief of the unknown world," as he called him, should receive such an honor. Mendoza is supposed to have said, "Matters may come to the cannon." Elizabeth is reported to have replied, "Another threat of that kind, and I'll fling you into a dungeon" (Douglas Bell, *Elizabethan Seamen* [Philadelphia: J. B. Lippincott, 1936], pp. 168–69).

43 The American version ends after Thorpe is knighted. Elizabeth's speech about preparing the nation for war and the closing visual transition from the forest of wooden mastheads to the steel superstructure of warships of 1940 were not used. In the British version, however, this material remained.

Production Credits

In charge of production	Jack L. Warner
Executive Producer	Hal B. Wallis
Associate Producer	Henry Blanke
Directed by	Michael Curtiz
Screenplay by	Howard Koch
	Seton I. Miller
Director of Photography	Sol Polito, A.S.C.
Art Director	Anton Grot
Dialogue Director	Jo Graham
Film Editor	George Amy
Sound by	Francis J. Scheid
Costumes by	Orry-Kelly
Makeup Artist	Perc Westmore
Special Effects by	Byron Haskin, A.S.C.
	H. F. Koenekamp, A.S.C.
Music Composed and Conducted by	Erich Wolfgang Korngold
Orchestrations by	Hugo Friedhofer
	Milan Roder
	Ray Heindorf
	Simon Bucharoff
Musical Director	Leo F. Forbstein
Fencing Master	Fred Cavens
Technical Advisers	Ali Hubert
	Thomas Manners
	William Kiel

Running time: 127 minutes
Released: August 1940

Cast

Geoffrey Thorpe	Errol Flynn
Doña Maria	Brenda Marshall
Don José Alvarez de Córdoba	Claude Rains
Sir John Burleson	Donald Crisp
Queen Elizabeth	Flora Robson
Carl Pitt	Alan Hale
Lord Wolfingham	Henry Daniell
Miss Latham	Una O'Connor
Abbott	James Stephenson
Captain López	Gilbert Roland
Danny Logan	William Lundigan
Oliver Scott	Julien Mitchell
King Philip II	Montagu Love
Eli Matson	J. M. Kerrigan
Martin Burke	David Bruce
William Tuttle	Clifford Brooke
Martin Barrett	Frank Wilcox
Walter Boggs	Clyde Cook
Eph Winters	Herbert Anderson
Inquisitor	Fritz Leiber
Ben Rollins	Edgar Buchanan
Monty Preston	Ellis Irving
Kroner	Francis McDonald
Arnold Cross	Charles Erwin
Captain Mendoza	Pedro de Cordoba
Peralta	Ian Keith
Lieutenant Ortega	Jack LaRue
Astronomer	Halliwell Hobbes
Captain Ortiz	Frank Lackteen
Chartmaker	Alec Craig
General Aguerra	Victor Varconi
Martin Frobisher	Robert Warwick
John Hawkins	Guy Bellis

Cast

Lieutenant	Lester Matthews
Slave master	Harry Cording
Drum beater	Art Miles
Slave master	Nestor Paiva
Sea Hawk	Michael Harvey
Native	Harry Silversmith
Maids of honor	Elizabeth Sifton
	Mary Anderson
Spanish officer	Gerald Mohr
Whippers	Dave Kashner
	J. W. Cody
	Anthony Warde

Appendix

The following scene was written by Seton I. Miller (Revised Temporary script, May 13, 1939). To compare it with Howard Koch's treatment of the same material, see pages 104–11.

123.   ANTEROOM   TRUCK SHOT   DAY

A small, beautifully furnished room. Camera discovers close shot of two chests brimming full of gold. As camera trucks back, Elizabeth is revealed standing near the chests, speaking to Thorpe.

QUEEN ELIZABETH:

. . . it is a goodly sight, but the use you ask for it is impossible. A new navy would only be a challenge to Spain. I know Philip too well. He would love such an excuse to build one of his own . . . many times as large.

THORPE:

One English sailing ship is the equal of any three plodding Spanish galleons.

The queen shakes her head, amused.

QUEEN ELIZABETH:

But not of seven or ten, Master Thorpe . . . and they can afford to build as many as they wish. King Philip receives more riches in one year from the West Indies than are in our treasury . . . including *all* that your stalwarts have given.

THORPE:

But if you were to receive that treasure supply instead, Majesty.

Appendix

124.　ELIZABETH　CLOSE-UP

The queen stares at this calm, surprising young man in outright amazement.

QUEEN ELIZABETH:
　What?!

125.　THORPE　CLOSE-UP

THORPE:
　Our plan is to bring it to England.

126.　AT TWO　MED. CLOSE

QUEEN ELIZABETH (impatiently):
　I begin to think that Wolfingham is right. You *are* mad. (Her curiosity gets the better of her.) What plan?

THORPE:
　The Spanish plate fleet collects all the treasure from the West Indies each year. It will be starting two months from now. With your permission we will sail in force and intercept it west of the Azores on its return.

QUEEN ELIZABETH:
　And have Spain waging war on us within a month!

THORPE (with swift earnestness):
　Better now than after years of preparation. She could not conquer us now . . . her forces are scattered from the Netherlands to Africa. But each passing year she will build ten ships to our one. Each victory will leave more forces free to attack us. The riches of the New World are her lifeblood. If only for one year we cut that lifeline and are first to build a fleet, England's shores will remain inviolate . . . Your throne secure, no matter what enemies plot against it! Majesty . . . I beg your sanction!

His fury conviction has swayed the queen, but she remains silent, a wavering indecision.

QUEEN ELIZABETH:
　You speak with conviction, Master Thorpe . . . but
　. . . (She shakes her head; flatly.) I cannot sanction
　any concerted action against the treasure fleet of
　Spain.

Thorpe is deeply disappointed, but still has hopes, and smiles.

THORPE:
　Would you deem it concerted action if the treasure
　were taken by one ship?

127.　QUEEN ELIZABETH　CLOSE SHOT
She looks at him, not knowing whether to be angry or amused.

QUEEN ELIZABETH:
　One ship? Preposterous.

128.　THORPE　CLOSE SHOT
He speaks with quiet assurance.

THORPE:
　But possible, Majesty. The richest part of it is
　brought across from Panama City to the fleet in the
　Caribbean Sea. It could be captured on the Isthmus.

129.　QUEEN ELIZABETH　CLOSE SHOT
She studies Thorpe gravely.

QUEEN ELIZABETH:
　You have such conviction in England's need of
　ships that you would risk your life in such an effort?

130.　AT TWO　MED. CLOSE
Thorpe speaks quietly.

THORPE:
> Willingly, Majesty.

QUEEN ELIZABETH:
> Sir John Robertson and the others share these beliefs?

THORPE:
> With their hearts and souls.

The queen is almost convinced.

QUEEN ELIZABETH:
> When would you sail?

THORPE:
> As soon as my ship is provisioned.

There is a pause.

QUEEN ELIZABETH:
> You have my permission.

Thorpe's face lights.

THORPE (eagerly):
> May I tell my friends that success will mean the building of a new fleet?

QUEEN ELIZABETH (a smile):
> You may tell them.

THORPE:
> Thank you, Majesty.

QUEEN ELIZABETH:
> Good fortune.

As she speaks she holds out her hand in dismissal. Thorpe kneels swiftly, kissing her hand in the customary gesture of placing his hands, one on the other, and placing them beneath her hand, raising it to his lips.

THORPE (with devoted respect):
> Majesty!

He rises and exits.

131. ANTEROOM MED. SHOT
as Thorpe swiftly exits, bowing again at door.

DISSOLVE TO:

132. PALACE GARDEN MED. CLOSE TRUCK SHOT

Inventory

The following materials from the Warner library of the Wisconsin Center for Film and Theater Research were used by Behlmer in preparing *The Sea Hawk* for the Wisconsin/Warner Bros. Screenplay Series:

Outline, "Beggars of the Sea," by Seton I. Miller. August 25, 1938. 25 pages.

Screenplay, "Beggars of the Sea," by Miller. No date. 175 pages.

Revised Temporary, by Miller. May 13, 1939. 158 pages.

Treatment, by Howard Koch. No date. 38 pages.

Final, [by Koch]. August 28 to September 21, 1939. 135 pages.

Revised Final, by Miller and Koch. January 23, 1940. 150 pages.

Second Revised Final, by Miller and Koch. January 30 with revisions to March 23, 1940. 160 pages.

DESIGNED BY GARY GORE
COMPOSED BY THE NORTH CENTRAL PUBLISHING COMPANY
ST. PAUL, MINNESOTA
MANUFACTURED BY INTER-COLLEGIATE PRESS, INC.
SHAWNEE MISSION, KANSAS
TEXT AND DISPLAY LINES ARE SET IN PALATINO

ᵂ

Library of Congress Cataloging in Publication Data
Koch, Howard.
The Sea Hawk.
(Wisconsin/Warner Bros. screenplay series)
Chiefly the screenplay by Howard Koch and Seton I. Miller,
based on the novel by Rafael Sabatini.
Bibliography: p. 43.
I. Behlmer, Rudy.   II. Miller, Seton I.
III. Sabatini, Rafael, 1875-1950. Sea-Hawk.
IV. Sea Hawk [motion picture]   V. Title.
PN1997.S319   791.43'72   81-70418
ISBN 0-299-09010-8   AACR2
ISBN 0-299-09014-0 (pbk.)

The Wisconsin/Warner Bros. Screenplay Series, a product of the Warner Brothers Film Library of the University of Wisconsin-Madison, offers scholars, students, researchers, and aficionados insights into individual films that have never before been possible.

The Warner library was acquired in 1957 by the United Artists Corporation, which in turn donated it to the Wisconsin Center for Film and Theater Research in 1969. The massive library, housed in the State Historical Society of Wisconsin, contains eight hundred sound feature films, fifteen hundred short subjects, and nineteen thousand still negatives, as well as the legal files, press books, and screenplays of virtually every Warner film produced from 1930 until 1950. This rich treasure trove has made the University of Wisconsin one of the major centers for film research, attracting scholars from around the world. This series of published screenplays represents a creative use of the Warner library, both a boon to scholars and a tribute to United Artists.

Most published film scripts are literal transcriptions of finished films. The Wisconsin/Warner screenplays are primary source documents—the final shooting versions including revisions made during production. As such, they reveal the art of screenwriting as other film transcriptions cannot. Comparing these screenplays with the final films will illuminate the arts of directing and acting, as well as the other arts of the film making process. (Films of the Warner library are available at modest rates from the United Artists nontheatrical rental library, United Artists/16 mm.)

From the eight hundred feature films in the library, the editors of the series selected for publication examples that have received critical recognition for excellence of directing, screenwriting, and acting, films distinctive in genre, in historical relevance, and in adaptation of well-known novels and plays.